Teaching
Stars and Performance

Jill Poppy

Series Editor: Vivienne Clark
Commissioning Editor: Wendy Earle

British Library Cataloguing-in-Publication Data
A catalogue record for this guide is available from the British Library

ISBN 1–84457–131–9

First published in 2006 by the British Film Institute
21 Stephen Street, London W1T 1LN

Design: Amanda Hawkes
Cover photograph: Gena Rowland in *Opening Night*, courtesy of *bfi* Stills
Printed in Great Britain by: Cromwell Press Ltd

www.bfi.org.uk
The British Film Institute's purpose is to champion moving image culture
in all its richness and diversity across the UK, for the benefit of as wide
an audience as possible, and to create and encourage debate.

Contents

Introduction to the series

Since the introduction of the revised post-16 qualifications (AS and A2 Level) in the UK in September 2000, the number of students taking A Level Film and Media Studies has increased significantly. For example, the latest entry statistics show the following trend:

Subject & Level	June 2001	June 2002	June 2005
A Level Film Studies+	2,017	–	–
AS Level Film Studies	3,852	–	9,188
A2 Level Film Studies	–	2,175	4,913
A Level Media Studies*+	16,293	–	–
AS Level Media Studies*	22,872	–	32,346
A2 Level Media Studies*	–	18,150	23,427

*Three combined awarding bodies' results
+Legacy syllabus – last entry June 2001
(Source: *bfi* Education website – AS/A2 statistics refer to cashed-in entries only)

In September 2006, a new A Level specification (syllabus), Moving Image Arts (offered by the Northern Ireland awarding body, CCEA) will be available throughout the UK and it is likely to attract even more students to this lively and popular subject area. In addition, changes to the 14–19 curriculum currently in development for 2008 will doubtless see further increases in take up of courses in this subject area.

Inevitably such increases in student numbers have led to a pressing demand for more teachers. But, given the comparatively recent appearance of both subjects at degree level (and limited availability of specialist post-graduate teaching courses), both new and experienced teachers from other disciplines are faced with teaching these subjects for the first time, without a degree-level background to help them with subject content and conceptual understanding.

In addition, these specifications saw the arrival of new set topics and areas of study, some of which change frequently, so there is a continued need for up-to-date resources to help teacher preparation.

I meet a large number of Film and Media Studies teachers every year in the course of my various roles and developed the concept and format of this series with the above factors, and busy and enthusiastic teachers, in mind. Each title provides an accessible reference resource, with essential topic content, as well as clear guidance on good classroom practice to improve the quality of teaching and students' learning. We are confident that, as well as supporting the teacher new to these subjects, the series provides the experienced specialist with new critical perspectives and teaching approaches as well as useful content.

The two sample schemes of work included in Section 1 are intended as practical models to help get teachers started. They are not prescriptive, as any effective scheme of work has to be developed with the specific requirements of an assessment context, and ability of the teaching group, in mind. Likewise, the worksheets provided in the online materials offer examples of good practice, which can be adapted to your specific needs and contexts. In some cases, the online resources include additional resources, such as interviews and illustrative material, available as webnotes. See www.bfi.org.uk/tfms.

The series is clear evidence of the range, depth and breadth of teacher expertise and specialist knowledge required at A Level in these subjects. Also, it is an affirmation of why this subject area is such an important, rich and compelling one for increasing numbers of 16- to 19-year-old students. Many of the more theoretical titles in the series include reference to practical exercises involving media production skills. It is important that it is understood here that the current A Levels in Media and Film Studies are not designed as vocational, or pre-vocational, qualifications. In these contexts, the place of practical media production is to offer students active, creative and engaging ways in which to explore theory and reflect on their own practice.

It has been very gratifying to see that the first titles in this series have found an international audience, in the USA, Canada and Australia, among others, and we hope that future titles continue to be of interest in international moving image education. Every author in the series is an experienced teacher of Film and/or Media Studies at this level and many have examining/moderating experience. It has been a pleasure to work so closely with such a diverse range of committed professionals and I should like to thank them for their individual contributions to this expanding series.

Vivienne Clark
Series Editor
April 2006

● Key features

- Assessment contexts for the major UK post-16 Film and Media Studies specifications
- Suggested schemes of work
- Historical contexts (where appropriate)
- Key facts, statistics and terms
- Detailed reference to the key concepts of Film and Media Studies
- Detailed case studies
- Glossaries
- Bibliographies
- Student worksheets, activities and resources (available online) – ready for you to print and photocopy for the classroom.

● Other titles available in the series include:

- *Teaching Scriptwriting, Screenplays and Storyboards for Film and TV Production* (Mark Readman);
- *Teaching TV Sitcom* (James Baker);
- *Teaching Digital Video Production* (Pete Fraser and Barney Oram);
- *Teaching TV News* (Eileen Lewis);
- *Teaching Women and Film* (Sarah Gilligan);
- *Teaching World Cinema* (Kate Gamm);
- *Teaching TV Soaps* (Lou Alexander and Alison Cousens);
- *Teaching Contemporary British Broadcasting* (Rachel Viney);
- *Teaching Contemporary British Cinema* (Sarah Casey Benyahia);
- *Teaching Music Video* (Pete Fraser);
- *Teaching Auteur Study* (David Wharton and Jeremy Grant);
- *Teaching Analysis of Film Language* (David Wharton and Jeremy Grant);
- *Teaching Men and Film* (Matthew Hall);
- *Teaching Film Censorship and Controversy* (Mark Readman).

● Forthcoming titles include:

- *Teaching Video Games*; *Teaching TV Drama*; *Teaching Short Films*.

SERIES EDITOR: Vivienne Clark is a former Head of Film and Media Studies and an Advanced Skills Teacher. She is currently an Associate Tutor of *bfi* Education and Principal Examiner for A Level Media Studies for one of the English awarding bodies. She is a freelance teacher trainer, media education consultant and writer/editor, with several published textbooks and resources, including *GCSE Media Studies* (Longman 2002), *Key Concepts and Skills for Media Studies* (Hodder Arnold 2002) and *The Complete A-Z Film and Media Studies Handbook* (Hodder & Stoughton 2006). She is also a course tutor for the *bfi*/Middlesex University MA module, An Introduction to Media Education.

AUTHOR: Jill Poppy has taught Film, Media Studies, Communication Studies and English at GCSE and A level. She has also taught Film Studies to undergraduates and set up GNVQ (ACVE) Intermediate and Advanced Media courses. She is Principal Examiner for A Level Film Studies and is a mentor for the British Film Institute panel of Associate Tutors. She has written a range of study guides, is a freelance teacher trainer, runs workshops and leads INSET courses for the British Film Institute and for the WJEC awarding body and other providers.

1

Introduction

Assessment contexts

Awarding body & level	Subject	Unit code	Module/Topic
✓ AQA AS Level	Media Studies	Med1	Reading the Media
✓ AQA AS Level	Media Studies	Med2	Textual Topics in Contemporary Media
✓ AQA A2 Level	Media Studies	Med4	Texts and Contexts in the Media
✓ AQA A2 Level	Media Studies	Med5	Independent Study
✓ OCR AS Level	Media Studies	2731	Textual Analysis
✓ OCR A2 Level	Media Studies	2734	Critical Research Study
✓ OCR A2 Level	Media Studies	2735	Media Issues and Debates
✓ WJEC AS Level	Media Studies	ME1	Modern Media Forms
✓ WJEC AS Level	Media Studies	ME2	Media Representations and Reception
✓ WJEC A2 Level	Media Studies	ME4	Investigating Media Texts
✓ WJEC A2 Level	Media Studies	ME5	Changing Media Industries
✓ WJEC AS Level	Film Studies	FS1	Making Meaning
✓ WJEC AS Level	Film Studies	FS2	Producers and Audiences
✓ WJEC AS Level	Film Studies	FS3	British and Irish Cinema
✓ WJEC A2 Level	Film Studies	FS4	Making Meaning 2
✓ WJEC A2 Level	Film Studies	FS5	Studies in World Cinema
✓ WJEC A2 Level	Film Studies	FS6	Critical Studies
✓ SQA Higher	Media Studies	D332	12 Media Analysis
✓ SQA Advanced Higher	Media Studies	D332	13 Media Analysis
✓ SQA Advanced Higher	Media Studies	D37A	13 Media Investigation

This guide is also relevant to the following specifications, as well as to international and Lifelong Learning courses:

- AQA, EdExcel, OCR – GNVQ and AVCE/Vocational A Level Media and Communication
- BTEC National Diploma.

The following titles in this series would be useful companions to this guide:

- *Teaching World Cinema* (Kate Gamm)
- *Teaching Women and Film* (Sarah Gilligan)
- *Teaching Men and Film* (Matthew Hall)
- *Teaching Auteur Study* (David Wharton and Jeremy Grant)
- *Teaching Analysis of Film Language* (David Wharton and Jeremy Grant)

In addition to its principal intended use as a guide for A Level teaching and equivalent international courses, some, or all, of this guide will be valuable at undergraduate level, particularly for students who have no previous experience of Film Studies at A2 Level. Teachers of GCSE Media Studies will also find this guide useful for their own preparation.

● Specification links

This study guide is relevant to the following specification areas, as well as to any study of media analysis, audiences, genre, institutions, contemporary British and American cinema, critical approaches to stars.

AQA AS Level Media Studies

- Med1 Reading the Media: Investigating and evaluating media language as one of the key foundation concepts.
- Med2 Textual Topics in Contemporary Media: The four topics include film and broadcast media which looks at film language and issues of audience and representation.
- Med4 Texts and Contexts in the Media: Representation of groups and stereotyping might be a useful approach to stars and performance.
- Med5 Independent Study: Stars and/or performance would serve well as a basis for research in contemporary media.

OCR AS Level Media Studies

- Unit 2731 Textual Analysis: Stars and performance as part of the deconstruction of the moving image medium.
- Unit 2734 Critical Research Study: Research topics include women and film, TV drama and world cinema, all of which could usefully include stars and performance.
- Unit 2735 Media Issues and Debates: Topics include contemporary British cinema and genre in film, both of which could focus on stars and performance.

WJEC AS Level Film Studies

- FS1 Making Meaning: Looking at how film communicates meaning both stylistically and formally; stars and performance as part of this analysis.
- FS2 Producers and Audiences: Understanding how cinema functions as an institution and its relationship with audiences.
- FS3 British and Irish Cinema: Identifying messages and values in British and Irish cinema.
- FS4 Making Meaning 2: Understanding film texts and spectatorship, authorship and traditions.
- FS5 Studies in World Cinema: Understanding of producers and audiences and the social and cultural context.
- FS6 Critical Studies: Evaluation of critical approaches, particularly through stars and performance.

WJEC AS Level Media Studies

- ME1 Modern Media Forms: Analysis of media texts; stars and performance as part of a system of signs.
- ME2 Media Representations and Reception: Looking at ideologies through the deconstruction of texts.
- ME4 Investigating Media Texts: Research skills and independent study; stars and performance as research topic.
- ME5 Changing Media Industries: Both the contemporary British film topic and institutional aspects of cinema could be served by the guide.

SQA Higher/Advanced Higher Media Studies

- D332 12 Media Analysis: Analysis of a range of texts such as cinema, print, advertising, TV.
- D332 13 Media Analysis: Application of media and film theory and debates to the analysis of a range of media texts such as cinema, print, advertising, TV.
- D37A 13 Media Investigation: Looking at audiences and consumption and gender representation in media texts.

Rationale: Why teach about stars and performance?

Stars are the most visible part of the film industry. They fascinate and engage film and media students and are a stimulating way of exploring a range of issues in Film and Media Studies. Audiences have responded to, and identified with, stars from the very beginning of the Hollywood studio days and stars have been created over the years in a variety of ways: through the films themselves and through other media constructions such as newspapers, magazines and fanzines, chatshows and websites.

This guide will investigate the meaning of stars in terms of media language and textual analysis, approaches to definitions of a star, stars and institutions, genre and marketing, audiences and fandom, spectatorship theories and stars and performance. Case studies will offer specific illustrations of aspects of these areas and there will be guidance for further investigation and development. An examination of performance will look at the contribution of technology to a cinematic performance; the expectations of the audience; differences between theatrical and cinema performance; issues of naturalism, presentation and representation and the connection between the star and the star performance.

How to use this guide

The sections of the guide can be used for various specifications and teachers may like to dip in and select the content and worksheets that they currently need. The materials in the guide have nearly all been tried out on media and film classes and have produced interesting responses and assignments. Studying stars can be a springboard for the following areas and the guide offers information and work for students on the following topics:

● **Reading stars as texts**

Star images can be perceived as being constructed not only from films and performances but from other texts which are constantly changing. The star image is the product of 'intertextuality', in which publicity, promotion, criticism and gossip interact with the film text. The star 'image' is contained in one person, which, together with the historical and social context, contributes to making particular meaning. This 'package' of ideological and connoted meanings is formed out of a series of signs which guide the audience towards the revelation of the 'truth' of the star, often in the merging of public and private worlds. Information and worksheets on this area can be found in the Critical approaches section (page 44) and also in the case studies.

● **Stars and the industry**

Stars have always been commodities that consistently draw audiences to films and 'star vehicles' have been constructed on the basis of the appeal of particular stars and performances which produce recognisable behaviour. The marketing of stars is one of the ways in which the industry attempts to ensure box-office returns – the star's financial success is also dependent upon his or her ability to give the audience pleasure. The studio system was central to the standardisation of the 'movie product' and stars were fixed with long contracts without much control over their roles. The studio system declined and the power of the star increased. Nowadays, we can still explore the relationship of stars with genres and directors and examine their more powerful roles both within the marketing of the film and in the production itself. The Hollywood section offers useful investigative worksheets on this topic and compares the film industries in Hollywood and Britain. The use of Hollywood's star personae in pre- and post-production stages can be usefully contrasted with the use and effect of stars in British filmmaking – an interesting way of contrasting two industries and two film cultures.

In a poll of 25,000, conducted by Channel 4 in May 2003 to establish the 100 greatest film stars, Al Pacino came top. The list was dominated by Hollywood tough men, with Anthony Hopkins the best-placed British actor in seventh place. The section on British film looks at this area in detail and the case studies on Hugh Grant and Mike Leigh offer information and worksheets on Britain and Hollywood both as competing and reflective institutions and in the context of stardom.

● Stars and spectatorship

An investigation of a range of critical approaches to spectatorship leads to an understanding of changes in perception and attitudes to stars. Ideas of spectatorship and audience identification allow us to explore the fragmented image of the star. We, the audience, piece together or construct this image to get the whole picture. Investigating fandom and the internet adds another dimension to the relationship of stars and their audiences. The students are asked to investigate ideas of fandom and spectatorship with reference to the case studies on Jennifer Aniston and Will Smith.

● Stars and performance

Screen performance raises issues of the construction of performance not just by the actor but by the camerawork, the editing and the *mise en scène*. Editing, for example, may be seen as limiting the expressive performance of an actor as filming outside of sequence can break the coherence of a performance. Physical movement on screen can be the main source of story information and the basis of our perception about characters. Looking at performance also involves seeing how Method acting challenged and changed mainstream Hollywood performance style. It brought a greater sense of realism to performances and a more complex sense of character. Mike Leigh's approach to performance is offered as a case study within the context of British cinema and can also be compared with the section on Method acting.

● Stars and representation

Stars offer a useful focus for understanding the key concept of representation through investigating who is being represented in terms of age, gender, class, religion, ethnicity and sexuality and how they are represented in terms of cultural and technical codes. The Will Smith case study is a specific focus; the Mike Leigh and Hugh Grant case studies also ask students to look at representations of class and Britishness.

Schemes of work

● Scheme of work 1: Definitions of stars and stars as texts

This four-week scheme of work is designed to introduce the idea of how stars are constructed, the idea of star and performer as an important part of film language and textual analysis leading teachers and students to investigate the meanings of stars and their performances in the film text. It can be introduced at AS Level as part of the work on textual analysis and then revisited at A2 where meanings in terms of history, context and performance can be more closely examined. This work can lead into several areas, some of which are suggested at the end of the scheme.

This scheme of work can be a useful springboard for:

● A comparison of British and American stars, asking students if they find any difference between the roles, publicity and marketing of these actors **Worksheet 11** asks students to examine the differences between American and British films in their use of stars. A case study could compare, for example, Jude Law and Brad Pitt or Keira Knightley and Angelina Jolie
● An examination of stars as texts (see Critical approaches (page 44) which examines stars as objects of desire and investigates issues of spectatorship and fandom; see also **Worksheet 13** and **Worksheet 6**)

Aims: To promote the idea of
● How stars are constructed
● Star and performer as an important component of film language and textual analysis
● Stars and their meanings
● The historical importance of stars

Outcomes:
● An analysis of a number of stars as texts with an indication of the meaning they bring to films
● A comparative analysis of particular stars
● A comparative analysis of particular stars from Britain and Hollywood

Week 1   Brainstorm what constitutes a star and what qualities are needed to be one
Worksheets 1 and **2**
Examine and discuss ideas of stardom: why are certain actors stars?
Worksheet 3

Week 2   Examine pictures of contemporary stars (eg Samuel L Jackson, Tom Hanks, Bruce Willis, Harrison Ford, Cameron Diaz, Keira Knightley, Brad Pitt, Johnny Depp)
Compare the 'meanings' they carry
Introduce Richard Dyer on Julia Roberts and Marilyn Monroe
Worksheet 12

Week 3   Review work on stars
Worksheets 14 and **15**
Watch film clips eg, from *Gladiator*, *Titanic*, *Die Hard*, *Charlie's Angels*, *Pulp Fiction* and *Pride and Prejudice* and discuss what alternative stars would be like in the main roles.

Week 4   Consolidation: Read three or four film synopses and identify possible stars for the main roles What different meanings (cultural codes) do the stars bring?
Discuss film language (technical codes) associated with particular stars

● Scheme of work 2: Mike Leigh and contemporary British cinema

This four-week scheme of work can be a useful introduction to auteur study or critical research at A2 Level or as part of investigating contemporary British cinema and realism at AS or A2. It is also useful for looking at film language and performance where you may like to compare how Mike Leigh works with his actors with the American Method. Other directions are suggested at the end of the scheme.

This scheme of work can be continued by:

● Comparing Mike Leigh's methods with the American Method,
Worksheet 19
● Comparing British and American films (see pages 37–43), looking in particular at Working Title or considering Mike Leigh's comments about British and American stars (see page 98) and whether his films fit a particular perception of 'Britishness', **Worksheet 21**

Aims: To promote the understanding of:
- Film language and performance
- Contemporary British cinema and realism
- Different approaches to actors and performance

Outcomes:
- A critical analysis of film language and how it constructs realism and authenticity
- A specific analysis of Mike Leigh's films and their construction
- An analysis of different styles of performance

Week 1   Show clips from 'social realist' British films (eg, *Kes*, *Raining Stones*, *The Full Monty*, *Lock Stock and Two Smoking Barrels*)
Discuss what they have in common in terms of film language and subject matter; ask students to suggest definitions of social realism
Watch and discuss opening sequences of *Life Is Sweet*, *Secrets and Lies* and *All or Nothing* **Worksheet 26**

Week 2   Discuss: What do Mike Leigh's films have in common and what do they share with the other films from Week 1?
Discuss Mike Leigh's background
Worksheet 25

Week 3   Performance: Discuss Imelda Staunton's comments (page 98)
Watch clips from Leigh's films, focusing on performance, eg photography sequences in *Secrets and Lies*
Worksheet 27

Week 4   Discuss and compare different styles of performance, eg Lillian Gish in *Broken Blossoms*, James Cagney in *Angels with Dirty Faces* – How do the performances fit with the subject matter of the films?
Worksheet 15

2

Background

Timeline

This selective timeline offers a background framework for understanding the development of stars as a phenomenon of film.

1908	The Motion Picture Patents Company (MPPC), known as the 'Trust', is set up and controlled by Thomas Edison.
1909	Rival production companies, including Carl Laemmle's Independent Motion Picture Company, are established to contest the MPPC's monopoly.
1910	Florence Lawrence, known as the Biograph girl, is established as a 'personality'.
1911	Los Angeles becomes the second most important production centre in America after New York.
1911–1913	Thomas Ince, a film director who worked at the Biograph Film Production Company, introduces a factory assembly line kind of production.
1915	*The Birth of a Nation* (US), directed and produced by D W Griffith, is a huge commercial success but is criticised for its racism. The MPPC is dissolved under anti-trust laws.
1919	United Artists is established by Douglas Fairbanks, Mary Pickford, Charlie Chaplin and D W Griffith.
1920s	The Kuleshov experiment.
1927	Warner Bros.' *The Jazz Singer* (Alan Crosland, US) is the first 'talkie' and Fox's Movietone the first sound newsreel.
1930s	Lee Strasberg and New York's Group Theatre introduces Stanislavski's Method.
1931	The Depression affects the industry and cinema attendances fall to 70 million a week.
1932	Attendance at the cinema in America falls to 55 million a week, with 4,000 cinemas closing.

1933	The Screen Actors Guild in America is established to guarantee actors a living wage.
1939	Hollywood's greatest year, with $187 million dollars spent on production and an average weekly cinema attendance of 85 million.
1939	David O Selznick produces *Gone with the Wind* (Victor Fleming, USA).
1945	The de Havilland decision against Warner Bros. marks the beginning of the decline of power in the studios.
1947	The Actors Studio is founded in New York by Elia Kazan.
1948	The Paramount Decree brings an end to motion picture industry monopolies.
1949	Paramount and RKO have to separate their theatres from production and distribution activities.
1949	Lee Strasberg becomes director of the Actors Studio.
1950s	James Stewart negotiates a different kind of deal: a share of the profits rather than a fee.
1958	RKO is bought by Desilu Productions.
1962	Talent agency Music Corporation of America (MCA) completes its takeover of Universal and Lew Wasserman becomes president.
1964	Sidney Poitier becomes the first African-American man to win an Academy Award as Best Actor in *Lilies of the Field*.
1965	The success of *The Sound of Music* (Robert Wise, USA) starts a run of high-budget productions.
1967	Warner Bros. is sold to Canadian television distributor Seven Arts, and then again to Warner Communications.
1971	Mike Leigh's first film, *Bleak Moments* (UK) is adapted from his stage play.
1972	The 'blaxploitation' cycle of films made by white producers aimed at African-American audiences reaches its peak with *Superfly* (Gordon Parks, Jr, USA, 1971).
1974	Box-office grosses increase in the USA by $150 million.
1975	Laura Mulvey's 'Visual Pleasure and Narrative Cinema' appears in *Screen*.
1979	The average film in America earns 80% of its receipts from theatrical release and 20% from video and television.
1982	Coca-Cola acquires Columbia who sells the studio to the Sony Corporation in 1989.
1986	Ted Turner sells MGM/UA back to Kerkorian but keeps its film and television library.
1986	British film producer David Puttnam briefly becomes chairman of Columbia.
1986	*Top Gun* (Tony Scott, USA), starring Tom Cruise, is released.

1987	Coca-Cola merges Columbia with Tri-Star to form Columbia Pictures Entertainment.
1990	Warner Communications is sold to the publisher Time, Inc., making it the largest entertainment company in the world.
1990s	The proliferation of a range of high-concept films such as *Con Air* (Simon West, USA) and *Face/Off* (John Woo, USA).
1990	Will Smith stars in NBC hit TV series, *The Fresh Prince of Bel-Air.*
1991	Richard Dyer analyses Julia Roberts as a star text.
1994	Paramount Communications sold to Viacom, Inc.
1994	*Four Weddings and a Funeral* (Mike Newell, UK) establishes Hugh Grant as an international star.
1994–2004	Jennifer Aniston plays Rachel in the hit TV series *Friends*.
2005	Mike Leigh is nominated for an Academy Award for Best Director for *Vera Drake*. Imelda Staunton won an Oscar for best actress and at the BAFTAs Mike Leigh won the David Lean award for direction.
2006	Philip Seymour Hoffman won the Oscar for best performance in *Capote*.

Hollywood, studios and stars

Most of the information in this section is drawn from Pam Cook and Mieke Bernink's *The Cinema Book* (1999) and Janet Staiger's *The Studio System* (1995).

● Screen identities

Most stars of the early feature period (1920s–40s) had such well-defined screen identities that they were virtually typecast. Theda Bara was the vamp, Mary Pickford was 'America's sweetheart', Tom Mix was a dandy and very different from the rough, straight-shooting William S Hart. To a greater degree than has been the case since, these stars were virtually genres unto themselves: Fairbanks was 'swashbuckling' and his films were 'swashbucklers'. When in 1919 he joined with Pickford, Chaplin and Griffith to found United Artists, he, like Chaplin and Pickford, was looking for more control, both economic and narrative, of his screen persona.

Ask students to name two or three actors who have clear screen identities today. Describe their identities and the genre of film they are associated with. Are these stars restricted to particular roles?

A useful follow-up to this discussion is to ask students to do **Worksheets 1 and 2: What is a star?** and **Worksheet 3: Legends and identities** which cover definitions of stardom, the roles that stars play in private and public life and extracts from an interview with Lauren Bacall where she challenges the definition of a screen legend.

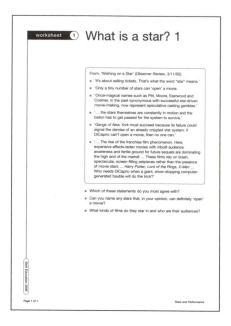

worksheet 1 — What is a star? 1

From: 'Wishing on a Star' (*Observer Review*, 3/11/02).

- 'It's about selling tickets. That's what the word "star" means.'
- 'Only a tiny number of stars can 'open' a movie.'
- 'Once-magical names such as Pitt, Moore, Eastwood and Costner, in the past synonymous with successful star-driven movie-making, now represent speculative casting gambles.'
- '… the stars themselves are constantly in motion and the baton has to get passed for the system to survive.'
- '*Gangs of New York* must succeed because its failure could signal the demise of an already crippled star system: if DiCaprio can't open a movie, then no one can.'
- '… The rise of the franchise film phenomenon. Here, expensive effects-laden movies with inbuilt audience awareness and fertile ground for future sequels are dominating the high end of the market … These films rely on brash, spectacular, screen-filling setpieces rather than the presence of movie stars … *Harry Potter*, *Lord of the Rings*, *X-Men* … Who needs DiCaprio when a giant, show-stopping computer-generated baddie will do the trick?'

- Which of these statements do you most agree with?
- Can you name any stars that, in your opinion, can definitely 'open' a movie?
- What kinds of films do they star in and who are their audiences?

© bfi Education 2006

Page 1 of 1 — Stars and Performance

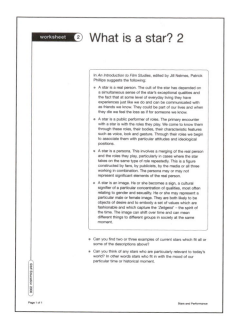

worksheet 2 — What is a star? 2

In *An Introduction to Film Studies*, edited by Jill Nelmes, Patrick Phillips suggests the following:

- A star is a real person. The cult of the star has depended on a simultaneous sense of the star's exceptional qualities and the fact that at some level of everyday living they have experiences just like we do and can be communicated with as friends we know. They could be part of our lives and when they die we feel the loss as if for someone we know.
- A star is a public performer of roles. The primary encounter with a star is with the roles they play. We come to know them through these roles, their bodies, their characteristic features such as voice, look and gesture. Through their roles we begin to associate them with particular attitudes and ideological positions.
- A star is a persona. This involves a merging of the real person and the roles they play, particularly in cases where the star takes on the same type of role repeatedly. This is a figure constructed by fans, by publicists, by the media or all three working in combination. The persona may or may not represent significant elements of the real person.
- A star is an image. He or she becomes a sign, a cultural signifier of a particular concentration of qualities, most often relating to gender and sexuality. He or she may represent a particular male or female image. They are both likely to be objects of desire and to embody a set of values which are fashionable and which capture the 'Zeitgeist' – the spirit of the time. The image can shift over time and can mean different things to different groups in society at the same moment.

- Can you find two or three examples of current stars which fit all or some of the descriptions above?
- Can you think of any stars who are particularly relevant to today's world? In other words stars who fit in with the mood of our particular time or historical moment.

© bfi Education 2006

Page 1 of 1 — Stars and Performance

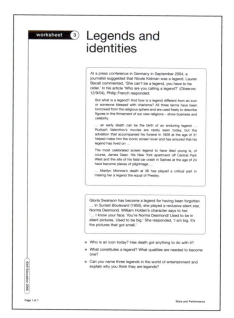

worksheet 3 — Legends and identities

At a press conference in Germany in September 2004, a journalist suggested that Nicole Kidman was a legend. Lauren Bacall commented, 'She can't be a legend, you have to be older.' In his article 'Who are you calling a legend?' (*Observer*, 12/9/04), Philip French responded:

But what is a legend? And how is a legend different from an icon or someone blessed with charisma? All three terms have been borrowed from the religious sphere and are used freely to describe figures in the firmament of our new religions – show business and celebrity.

… an early death can be the birth of an enduring legend. Rudolph Valentino's movies are rarely seen today, but the adulation that accompanied his funeral in 1926 at the age of 31 helped make him the iconic screen lover and has ensured that his legend has lived on …

The most celebrated screen legend to have died young is, of course, James Dean. His New York apartment off Central Park West and the site of his fatal car crash in Salinas at the age of 24 have become places of pilgrimage …

… Marilyn Monroe's death at 36 has played a critical part in making her a legend the equal of Presley.

Gloria Swanson has become a legend for having been forgotten … In *Sunset Boulevard* (1950), she played a reclusive silent star, Norma Desmond. William Holden's character says to her: '… I know your face. You're Norma Desmond! Used to be in silent pictures. Used to be big.' She responded, 'I am big. It's the pictures that got small.'

- Who is an icon today? Has death got anything to do with it?
- What constitutes a legend? What qualities are needed to become one?
- Can you name three legends in the world of entertainment and explain why you think they are legends?

© bfi Education 2006

Page 1 of 1 — Stars and Performance

To access student worksheets and other online materials go to *Teaching Stars and Performance* at **www.bfi.org.uk/tfms** and enter User name: **stars@bfi.org.uk** and Password: **te1302sp**.

© Corel Corporation

● Hollywood: the beginnings

Hollywood's most successful period is usually identified as the years when the studio system flourished (approximately 1930–55) and 1939 is often pinpointed as its finest year. This was the period when the film industry prospered as an oligopoly: the production of films was dominated almost entirely by a small number of vertically integrated companies. Vertical integration meant that film companies (the studios) held controlling interests in the distribution and exhibition as well as the production of films. The consolidation and success of this system can be dated from around 1930 but its roots can be traced back to the 'assembly line' methods of filmmaking introduced as early as 1913.

In the USA many of the early film pioneers were first- or second-generation immigrants who started as exhibitors in the Eastern cities often owning nickelodeons (a 'nickel-Odeon' was often just a converted store or saloon where audiences were charged a nickel – five cents – to watch films). By 1910 these exhibitors had begun to construct more grandiose, purpose-built theatres to accommodate the demands of middle-class audiences for better facilities. The popularity of the new medium prompted them to expand into the production side of films.

Hollywood was an ideal location for this new film industry – land was cheap, the climate was reliable (filmmaking was a mainly outdoor activity at this time), labour was cheap, the natural light was good, settings were varied and it was a long way from the Eastern states where the Motion Picture Patents Company (MPPC), known as the 'Trust', was trying to insist on licence fees for production and projection equipment. The MPPC was set up in 1908 as cinema was becoming hugely popular and profitable. Controlled by Thomas Edison, it was a coalition of the major production companies who were keen to control all aspects of the film industry. The relocation to Hollywood was a result of the discontent of independent producers who, in 1915, sued the MPPC under anti-trust laws.

● The studio system

The development of the Hollywood studio system during the 1910s and 1920s and the accompanying American dominance of world film markets were among the most significant developments in cinema history. The events in these years defined standard commercial filmmaking. Some of the companies from this era are still making films and the division of labour into specialised tasks has continued to the present day.

Between 1911 and 1913 Thomas Ince, a film director, who worked at Biograph Film Production Company, introduced a film production practice more in line with how other industries functioned, rather like an assembly line in a factory. This new approach saw the separation of planning and production and by 1915 he had six writers, nine directors and six shooting units. There were ten other departments in the studio based upon separate work functions, for example, photography, set making, costumes, cutting, music. Hollywood film studios produced films in the way factories produced cars but each product was different. This system has often been compared with industrial assembly line manufacture, in which a manager supervises a number of workers, each repeating a particular task at a particular rate in a fixed order. This division of labour meant different people all worked as part of a team to produce a finished film. The studio system of production is divided into three stages:

- Pre-production: planning, writing the script, storyboarding, casting, planning filming, recruiting technical crews, commissioning costumes, finding locations and so on;
- Production: shooting the film;
- Post-production: assembling and editing the film, adding titles and sound.

Filmmaking developed and grew in strength and projects became more ambitious. One of the most important filmmakers of this time was D W Griffith, also working at Biograph. He became famous for making huge extravaganzas, requiring large sets, large casts and many costumes and props, employing a large labour force.

The eight studios

By 1930 eight large companies dominated the industry. The Hollywood oligopoly had settled into a structure that did not change very much for nearly 20 years.

First there were the majors, often called the 'Big Five': Paramount, Loews/MGM, Fox, which became 20th Century-Fox in 1935, Warner Bros. and RKO. To be a major, the company had to be vertically integrated – they made, released and marketed their films and owned a theatre chain. Exhibition was the most profitable sector of the film industry and box-office receipts were how studios recouped the cost of making films. The film studios wanted these profits for themselves. They did not own all the cinemas in the US but the ones that they did own were 'first-run' cinemas that got the most popular films before their competitors (as a result they delivered 75% of all theatrical revenues).

Smaller companies with few or no exhibition centres formed the minors or the 'Little Three': Universal, Columbia and United Artists. There were also independent producers such as Walt Disney and Samuel Goldwyn.

The majors (vertically integrated)

- *MGM*: Louis B Mayer was the head of production in this studio and the role of the producer was emphasised. Mervyn LeRoy (a director from Warner Bros.) joined MGM to become a producer and in 1939 made *The Wizard of Oz* (Victor Fleming, USA). It was expensive to make and not a major hit and showed a loss on its first release. The studio became known as the 'home of glitz and glamour, of the musical and the American Dream'. The studio's stars included Greta Garbo, Clark Gable and Spencer Tracy.
- *Paramount*: In the early 1930s Paramount was known for its European-style productions. Josef von Sternberg made films with Marlene Dietrich there. The studio also relied on comedy and vaudeville performers and the Marx Brothers made their earliest films there, such as *Duck Soup* (Leo McCarey, USA). Bob Hope and Bing Crosby became box-office attractions for this studio, as well as Gary Cooper. In the 1930s and 40s producer/director Cecil B de Mille worked there on big budget historical films; his 1939 epic *Union Pacific* (USA) was very popular.
- *Fox*: In the late 1920s Fox made its name with prestige productions such as *Sunrise* (F W Murnau, USA, 1927). However, this type of production overstretched the company badly. In 1935 it joined with 20th Century Pictures to become 20th Century-Fox, headed by Darryl F Zanuck. It had five very popular stars – Will Rogers, Tyrone Power, Alice Faye, Sonja Henie (a Norwegian skating star) and Shirley Temple.

- *Warner Bros.*: This company made modest but predictable profits on a relatively large number of low-budget films. It led the way in introducing sound to the cinema. Badly hit by the Depression, it adhered to assembly line methods with rigid production schedules and low budgets. Its sets were smaller than MGM and its popular actors – James Cagney, Bette Davis, Humphrey Bogart and Errol Flynn – worked in more films. The studio concentrated on creating popular genres and producing them over and over again – Busby Berkeley musicals, gangster films and a collection of films which focused on working-class figures.
- *RKO*: In the early 1930s this studio undertook large, ambitious projects such as *King Kong* (Merian C Cooper, USA) and the sophisticated musical comedies of Fred Astaire and Ginger Rogers. The money required to sustain these projects and the buildings of the RKO showcase cinema (the Radio City Music Hall with 6,200 seats) meant that they overstretched themselves financially. In 1939 RKO signed a contract with Orson Welles, then a celebrated radio and stage producer, to write, direct and produce one film a year with total freedom after the final script was approved. *Citizen Kane* (Orson Welles, USA, 1941) became the most important RKO film but it did not take much money at the time of its release. RKO is often known as the 'studio without a style' perhaps because of its constant change in management.

The minors

- These did not control exhibition but had access to the majors' exhibition/theatrical circuit.
- *Universal:* Most famous for their production of horror films in the early 1930s, popular possibly because audiences during the Depression wanted escapist entertainment. The visual style of early horror offered an easy transition from silent movies to sound, and sequels could run and run. Boris Karloff and Bela Lugosi were big stars for the studio, which also employed talented technicians including cameramen, directors, make-up artists and set designers, many of whom had graduated from the school of classic German silent film.
- *Columbia:* During the 1930s Columbia's low-budget supporting features for double bills (70 minutes running time – few or no stars) accounted for 70% of their annual output. In this way they were less affected by the financial problems of the large studios. They occasionally invested in more expensive films, such as Frank Capra's big hit *It Happened One Night* (USA, 1934). They did not have their own big stars but they borrowed from other studios. By the end of the 1930s a policy was established of bringing in outside stars and directors and paying them percentage deals. Several major directors, such as John Ford and George Cukor, worked briefly for Columbia, enjoying the fact they could direct and produce their own films.

Howard Hawks made *His Girl Friday* (USA, 1940) at Columbia with Cary Grant and Rosalind Russell, and Rita Hayworth was developed into a big star there.

- *United Artists:* The coming of sound brought about a slow decline in this studio, set up and owned by D W Griffith, Charlie Chaplin, Mary Pickford, Douglas Fairbanks and Samuel Goldwyn. They all retired in the early to mid-1930s. Charlie Chaplin released a feature once every five years. The company released *The Private Life of Henry VIII* (Alexander Korda, UK, 1933), some of Hitchcock's American films and some of William Wyler's. Producer Walter Wanger's *Stagecoach* (John Ford, USA, 1939) was its most successful film.

The producer and the director

> The way I see it, my function is to be responsible for everything (David O Selznick, producer, *Gone with the Wind*).

Although we now think of the director as the principal creator of the film, in the 1930s producers and stars would have been considered the major factors in each production. Producers like Irving Thalberg, Hal Wallis and Darryl F Zanuck left strong imprints on films and they carefully nurtured actors such as Katharine Hepburn, Clark Gable, Marlene Dietrich and James Stewart. The producer was a key figure, supervising a studio's films and responsible for studio identity. He had to maintain regular output and quality within a budget. The basic tool for planning was the continuity script, which specified details such as shot breakdown, *mise en scène* and budget. The associate producer was the only person who saw the film through the complete process – he monitored shooting schedules, budgets etc. The prime concern was that the films ran to schedule and budget. The associate producers were answerable to the head of production, who was responsible for making sure that the studio made money. All those involved with making the film (other than the producer) were salaried staff with particular and limited functions.

The director was sometimes merely a supervisor who oversaw the recording of images and sounds. His role was limited to organising the day-to-day filming with little say over the final product. The director would exercise some control over the script, costume etc but much of the creativity was the responsibility of departmental experts in the planning stage, in line with what the producer wanted. A director would be given a project only after a writing team had finished the screenplay. Other personnel would be selected for him and once the film had been shot, the project would pass to the editors.

Hollywood films over the decades have been both useful and entertaining in their own representations of Hollywood's history, technological developments and attitudes to stars:

● **Films about film** These films document shifts in production and distribution and in the relationships between filmmakers. Made in the genres of comedy melodrama they are provide entertaining introductions on how films were made:

- *Sunset Boulevard* (Billy Wilder, USA, 1950) illustrates the fate of a faded star, played by Gloria Swanson. It shows the impact of sound on silent movie stars, and emphasises the importance of the close-up. The increase in the use of the close-up was important in changing the style of filmmaking and to the emerging star system.

- *The Bad and the Beautiful* (Vincente Minnelli, USA, 1952) illustrates the roles and relationships of the producer, director, writer and actor. The opening sequences of the film offer an excellent example of a Hollywood studio set.

- *Singin' in the Rain* (Gene Kelly and Stanley Donen, USA, 1952) offers an amusing look at the effect the introduction of sound had on audiences and stars.

- *A Star is Born* (George Cukor, USA, 1954) looks at the ruin of careers and the vicious characters in the industry such as the press agent; the film stars Judy Garland – herself a victim of the studio system.

- In contrast, Robert Altman's *The Player* (USA, 1992) looks at Hollywood today and illustrates how films are 'packaged' and 'pitched'.

- *Living in Oblivion* (Tom DiCillo, USA, 1995) shows the workings, relationships and difficulties of an independent, low-budget film crew.

Worksheet 4: Studios and stars
asks students to investigate and produce a case study of a studio, director, producer or actor from this era (1930–55).

To access student worksheets and other online materials go to *Teaching Stars and Performance* at **www.bfi.org.uk/tfms** and enter User name: **stars@bfi.org.uk** and Password: **te1302sp**.

● The emergence of the star system

Information in this section is drawn from *The Cinema Book* (1999), *The Studio System* (1995) and an essay by Brian Gallagher 'Some Historical Reflections on the Paradoxes of Stardom in the American Film Industry, 1910–1960' (www.imagesjournal.com).

Making stars

In the early days of filmmaking, the technological spectacle took precedence over identification with character. However, as filmmaking increasingly took character as the central focus of narrative, Hollywood became very good at creating a mythic screen image of a star as a rare, intense and, usually, beautiful individual. From the rise of the star system in around 1910, American cinema stars on screen represented individuals able to command the narrative subservience of a large community of 'supporting players'. Brian Gallagher suggests that off screen the star embodied a cultural paradigm – a worker acknowledged as separate and superior both by co-workers and by the moviegoing public, a person willingly granted privileged status in both the local community (Hollywood) and in the wider culture.

Gallagher reports that one of the stories circulating about the MPPC (Motion Picture Patents Company) in the early 20th century was that it refused to reveal the identities of its actors to prevent them from gaining recognition and asking for large salaries. Thus it was allegedly independent producers who invented the practice of publicising their feature players, imitating current theatrical practices in which stars, touring with their own ensemble companies, ruled the day. The public's thirst for knowledge about their favourite players may have contributed to the downfall of the MPPC, although many MPPC members had begun exploiting their stars. In 1909, Edison introduced stock players in Vitagraph's catalogues, with long descriptions of their prior experiences and successes on stage. At this stage the studios were keen to push their own names and keep control of the branding of their own products. They kept the nicknames 'The Biograph Girl' and 'The Vitagraph Girl' but the girls were interchangeable.

Typical was Carl Laemmle's poaching of the Biograph girl, Florence Lawrence, in 1910 for his Independent Motion Picture Company. After spreading the story that she had been killed in a streetcar accident, Laemmle produced Florence Lawrence who, after that, appeared under her own name in his pictures. The independents were also more willing to move into the production of longer and feature-length films, a move which coincided with the fuller exploitation of the potential of stars in such films.

- Students may like to investigate D W Griffith, a leading innovator in the industry, both as an independent director and in terms of his relationship with stars. His defection from Biograph to the new Mutual in 1913 was clearly a sign that the independent production companies with their riskier, more innovative management style were carrying the day. Within two years he made *The Birth of a Nation*, which fixed at least three 'stars' in the public consciousness: Lillian Gish, Mae Marsh and Griffith himself.

Marketing stars

The championing of individual players quickly became a key part of the marketing strategy that underpinned the eight-company monopoly (Laemmle's company became Universal, Zukor's Paramount). As Gallagher points out,

> From a business point of view, there are many advantages in the star system. The star has tangible features which can be advertised and marketed – a face, a body, a pair of legs, a voice, a certain kind of personality, real or synthetic – and can be typed as the wicked villain, the honest hero, the fatal siren, the sweet young girl, the neurotic woman. The system provides a formula easy to understand and has made the production of movies seem more like just another business. The use of this formula may serve also to protect the executives from talent and from having to pay much attention to such intangibles as the quality of the story or of the acting. Here is a standardized product which can be advertised and sold, and which not only they, but also banks and exhibitors, regard as insurance for large profits.

- Ask students to compare these comments with the description of today's high-concept films in the section on contemporary Hollywood. What are the similarities?

Star vehicles

Star vehicles were not only sold directly to the public (in theatres owned by the studios) but were also sold to independent theatre owners, who were often at the mercy of studios intent on packaging their lesser wares along with their premium goods. Adolph Zukor was the man who invented block-booking, by insisting that these independent theatre owners take the whole Paramount list to get features starring the likes of Mary Pickford. The policy was much imitated, especially in the 1930s, when double bills became a major strategy in fighting declining Depression audiences. Studios like Warner Bros., with a limited roster of stars, were able to negotiate these stars into bigger profits by making them the centre of a whole block-booking operation: to get Cagney or Davis or Errol Flynn films, the independent theatre owner had to accept some weak 'A' films and a fair share of 'B' films. In a sense these stars were helping to support a whole production schedule over which they had little knowledge and no control – they certainly had no control over the exploitation of their performance.

Popular new stars like Rudolph Valentino, Greta Garbo and John Gilbert rose in the 1920s. By then the three major comedy stars of the late 1910s – Chaplin, Lloyd and Keaton – had also moved into feature-film production, confirming their star status by putting themselves in 'star-length' vehicles. A more recent example of film as star vehicle is *Beverly Hills Cop* (Martin Brest, USA, 1984). Originally written as an action thriller with Sylvester Stallone in the lead, the film was re-scripted as an action-comedy when they decided to cast Eddie Murphy instead.

Worksheet 5: Star vehicles asks students to consider contemporary star vehicles and to consider what pleasures they provide audiences today.

To access student worksheets and other online materials go to *Teaching Stars and Performance* at **www.bfi.org.uk/tfms** and enter User name: **stars@bfi.org.uk** and Password: **te1302sp**.

Publicity

Parallel to the foregrounding of individual film players was the creation of an accompanying printed and graphic discourse about them – in newspapers and magazines, but also on products ranging from slides, trade photos and lobby cards to cigarette packs. Probably the most influential were the fan magazines, which brought stars into the home by making their images portable and which allowed the audience to enter actively into the discourse on stardom by reprinting fan letters. The earliest fan magazines, *Motion Picture Story* and *Photoplay* were founded in 1911, as short-fiction magazines, trading on the increasing popularity of films and film stars. They contained plot synopses, star portraits, editorial columns and letters to the editor. The ultimate purpose of these magazines was to sell films, and articles were often written by studio publicists.

Brian Gallagher refers to Richard de Cordova who suggests that around 1914 'the private lives of the stars emerged as a new site of knowledge and truth.' Fan magazines and other public vehicles in the classical age fulfilled the vital function of authenticating the star's existence in the real world, even though the boundaries were blurred. A significant portion of this fan discourse centred on home and family – with the star photographed surrounded by family members, in his/her tastefully lavish home – a centring that at once related the star to the similar elements (home, family) in the fan's life and, at the same time, elevated the star through his or her beauty, fame, wealth and possessions, far above the fan. In this respect the magazine discourse played on the same presence/absence that many have identified at the heart of cinema itself. (*Picture Personalities: The Emergence of the Star System in America*, 1990, cited by Brian Gallagher)

The fan magazine and other kinds of publicity materials lifted the images of the stars out of cinemas and circulated them into general culture:

> The effect of the fan magazines and various and other types of publicity was to forge a link between the specialized arena, the movie theatre, and all the arenas of everyday activity (the home, the office, modes of public transportation). Fans could read about and possess images both mental and visual of their favourite stars – closely related to but distinct from the way that they related to the stars' images on the screen. (Hortense Powdermaker, *Hollywood: the Dream Factory*, 1951, cited by Brian Gallagher)

The fan discourse of magazines and newspapers sometimes became a forum for the stars' discontent, with the rebellious independence of these stars turned into a positive part of their total image. The rise of gossip columnists like Louella Parsons and Hedda Hopper, who became very powerful in Hollywood, meant that millions of people a day read about the stars in contexts that could only be partially controlled by industry forces. By the 1920s there were more than a dozen major fan magazines, with *Photoplay*'s circulation running to over 2 million.

Brian Gallagher states that:

> The unprecedented rise of the fan magazine's popularity in the 1920s took place within a broader ideological framework marked by women's growing economic and sexual emancipation and the widespread belief that changes in women's behaviour were contributing to a radical subversion of American gender ideals ... in comparison with general cultural discourse aimed at men ... often evidenced a progressive view of women's changing sexual and economic roles.

In 1923 a writer in *Photoplay* positioned women, otherwise politically inconsequential, as the arbiters of stardom … 'at the box office her two-bit ballot controls the situation, making and unmaking stars.' This idea may explain the screen power of a Valentino at the time.

Worksheet 6: **Stars and the discourse of fandom** asks students to consider this subject in more detail and to choose a star for a case study, collecting stories from a range of publicity and fan material. They are asked to look at how this material reinforces and contributes to our perception of the star.

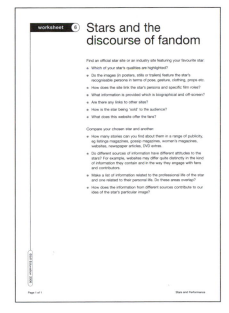

To access student worksheets and other online materials go to *Teaching Stars and Performance* at **www.bfi.org.uk/tfms** and enter User name: **stars@bfi.org.uk** and Password: **te1302sp**.

Studios, stars and contracts

Each major studio had its own stable of stars held under contract to make a certain number of films. Although some stars could command high salaries under this system, it also demanded large sacrifices. Loyalty to the studio was all-important and careers could be ruined if stars tried to break their contracts. Bette Davis described this system as offering 'the security of prison'. Penalties were added to the end of contracts so actors could be trapped for 10 or 15 years working off what was originally a seven-year contract. Some stars fought to get a better deal for themselves and formed their own companies: Charlie Chaplin, Douglas Fairbanks and Mary Pickford became founders of United Artists. This was a significant early milestone in the rise of 'star power'.

In 1933 actors were earning approximately $15 a day and the Screen Actors Guild was founded to guarantee a living wage and a supportive working environment. Stars were working unrestricted hours and had no enforced meal breaks; they had seven-year contracts that they could not break and which they were forced to renew for a studio which could also dictate their lifestyle and the political opinions they could express. The climate at the time was anti-labour and it took some courage to join a union. Members had to use passwords, backdoors and secret meeting places to elude studio detectives. Major stars had fame and money and studio executives had little fame (David O Selznick being an exception) but total control. The star's only weapon was a refusal to work, which meant suspension. Suspension was one of the harshest punishments that the studios meted out to their stars. It meant that anyone who refused to play a particular role was obliged to wait, unpaid, while the film was shot and then half that time again. This time penalty was then added to the end of their contract thus trapping the actors. It took until 1937 for the studios to accept the Guild's jurisdiction.

The end of the studio system

But while the Guild had won actors better working conditions, the studios still basically 'owned' their stars – there was a tacit agreement among studios not to raid each other for talent and actors. This restrictive environment was challenged by the actions of four major stars.

Olivia de Havilland filed a suit against Warner Bros. in 1943. Warner Bros. had loaned Olivia de Havilland to David O Selznick for *Gone with the Wind*, in which she played Melanie Wilkes, but after she returned to Warner Bros., they kept offering her insignificant roles. She turned these down and she was given a six-month suspension. She felt that the persistent extension of her contract was unfair practice and she challenged this in the courts – and won. As a direct result all future studio contracts were limited to a maximum of seven consecutive years regardless of any suspension and contracts were frequently re-negotiated. The landmark 'de Havilland decision' in 1945, which ended the term contract system, produced the catalyst which many saw as the beginning of the decline of the power of the major Hollywood studios. Although she was absent from the screen for the three years of the court case, Olivia de Havilland celebrated her return with an Oscar-winning performance for Paramount in *To Each His Own* (Mitchell Leisen, USA, 1946).

A few years later, the Supreme Court dealt another fatal blow to the studios in its anti-trust Paramount Decree, which ended motion picture industry monopolies, clearing the way for independents to enter the trade. Suddenly actors had the power to control their own careers.

Bette Davis was at Warner Bros. from 1931 to 1948 and was in conflict with them the whole time she was there. She regularly accepted suspensions and fought for better parts (and more money). In 1936 she filed suit against

Warners claiming that her contract was a form of 'slavery'. She lost the case but she was not punished, rather rewarded for her rebellion. Immediately after the court case, Jack Warner bought her the film *Jezebel* (William Wyler, USA, 1938). In later years Warner Bros. gave her her own independent corporation and 35% of the net profits from her pictures to keep her working at the studio. She came to be widely and positively regarded as an individual who successfully managed to buck the system. She has also come to be seen as a courageous woman and film star who stood for rebellion against male authority, demanded control over her work and struggled for artistic integrity and autonomy. Bette Davis's first picture as a non-contract player was significant. She played the independent, compelling stage actress Margo Channing in *All About Eve* (Joseph L Mankiewicz, USA, 1950). The film, to some extent, reflected her career with characters exploiting her talent and taking advantage of her independent ways. (We will look more closely at Bette Davis's influence and performance in the section on Performance, pages 57 and 62.)

James Cagney worked for Warner Bros. and complained that no matter how large his salary (considerably higher than any other star by 1938), he was unable to share in the profits of films that did particularly well. He was often dissatisfied with the writers and directors the studio assigned to his films, as well as with many of his leading ladies. Also, he believed that the studio was conspiring to typecast him in gangster parts.

In 1936 when he was making $4,500 a week, the studio withheld $1,500 of that for illness and bad behaviour. Also, Warner Bros. refused to lend him out, which meant he had little chance to expand his repertoire of roles. He won a court order against Warner Bros. (for not paying him his market value) and was released from his contract. He left to work for an independent production company, which was unsuccessful, but returned to Warner Bros. in a much better position than before. He agreed to make 11 pictures for the studio – two or three per year for the next five years. In return, he was to receive $150,000 per picture plus 10% of the grosses over $1,500,000. Twelve weeks of continuous vacation were guaranteed and also a 'happiness' clause, which meant that he could cancel his contract after any picture or at the end of any given year if his relationship with the studio was 'obnoxious or unsatisfactory to him'. This was a contract that all stars would have liked. He was given a good deal more input on the films he made for the studio. The first of these was *White Heat* (USA, 1949), directed by Raoul Walsh, where he received recognition that he had raised the gangster role to an archetype. (James Cagney's performances are compared with Method acting in the section on Performance, page 65.)

By 1955 **James Stewart** had become Hollywood's top box-office star. For the films he made with Universal, which were nearly all hits, Stewart took 50% of the profits rather than a salary – a deal negotiated for him by his agent, Lew Wasserman. At Universal, Stewart starred in a number of Westerns which played to the neurotic side of his persona first fully exhibited in *It's a Wonderful Life* (Frank Capra, USA, 1947). His contract with Universal was non-exclusive so Lew Wasserman (MCA) was able to arrange for him to star in three highly visible and highly profitable Hitchcock films: *Rear Window* (USA, 1954), *The Man Who Knew Too Much* (USA, 1956) and *Vertigo* (USA, 1958). Stewart epitomises the freelance star of the 1950s who, supported by a powerful agent, was able to gain some measure of artistic control and to maximise his earning potential. His success reflects the new structures of control in Hollywood and the changing tastes of the film audience. In steering Stewart through 1950s' Hollywood, a period in which television was eating away at box-office revenues year by year, Wasserman was more like a producer than an agent in the older sense – he was more powerful than any real producer in the decade.

This kind of deal had advantages for star and studio: for the star, the deal could potentially raise his cumulative earning power; for the studio, the deal allowed Universal to employ a major star without paying up-front or at all if the film failed at the box office. This was not the first profit-participation deal but it was the most successful one. The deal made the issue of participation and the right of approval key areas in the new market of star labour.

The star system redefined

Today, the freedom and power for stars brought about by the demise of the studio system is evident in the fact that many stars have their own production companies becoming, in essence, their own mini-studios. The actor who produces, directs and initiates his/her own projects is no longer a phenomenon but an accepted part of the industry. From very small beginnings the Screen Actors Guild and its representatives have become a powerful voice for performers. It now has 20 branches across the US.

During the late 1940s and 1950s as the studio system was gradually dismantled, the most powerful agency in Hollywood was the Music Corporation of America (MCA), founded in 1924 by Dr Jules Stein, as a booking agent for bands. In 1936, after moving to Hollywood, Stein hired Lew Wasserman as an agent, who quickly established his skill in brokering powerful deals for MCA film and music clients. In 1946 Wasserman became president of the corporation, guiding MCA through the years of upheaval in Hollywood.

MCA's power was built on the impressive list of stars it represented. In 1959, these included Carroll Baker, Ernest Borgnine, Marlon Brando, Leslie Caron, Montgomery Clift, Joseph Cotten, Joan Crawford, Tony Curtis, Dorothy Dandridge, Clark Gable, Charlton Heston, William Holden, Boris Karloff,

Howard Keel, Charles Laughton, Jack Lemmon, Dean Martin, Marilyn Monroe, Gregory Peck, Anthony Perkins, Jane Russell, Joanne Woodward and Jane Wyman. MCA packaged film projects that brought together the agency's talents. For example, for *Some Like It Hot* (USA, 1959), MCA packaged the director Billy Wilder with the film's stars, Tony Curtis, Jack Lemmon and Marilyn Monroe.

Backed by the agency's star list MCA was able to aggressively pursue beneficial deals for individual clients. As we have already seen, in 1950 Wasserman used the influence of MCA to broker a key deal between Universal and James Stewart, for the star's work on *Winchester '73* (Anthony Mann, USA, 1950). The deal granted the star a participating share in profits from the film. Profit participation went back to the days when Mary Pickford had personally earned half the gross box-office receipts from her films. Similar terms were agreed in the 1930s by Mae West and the Marx Brothers.

MCA had started several of the trends that redefined the star system following the reorganisation of the studios. It had played the role of packager, using its impressive list of stars to develop productions. Deals such as the one struck for James Stewart had exploited new possibilities in the earning power of stars in the freelance labour market. It was MCA that also saw the potential that the new popularity of television offered as a window for star talent.

Stars today

In *The Whole Equation, A History of Hollywood*, David Thomson (2005) looks at the Nicole Kidman's career, her Oscar for *The Hours*, and the relationship she has with studios and publicists:

> Once upon a time, a studio would have owned Nicole Kidman, and promoted her out of the same office over a stretch of years, now she is her own mistress. And as she moves from project to project, from one studio to another, she needs more comfort than that carousel offers. So she engages a public relations company, and she has someone who 'handles' her, on a retainer basis. That person is intimately involved in the mysterious image and identity of a star.

David Thomson's account of the history of Hollywood is informed, detailed, passionate and engaged: highly recommended.

In terms of the changing power of the stars students may also like to consider the careers of Clint Eastwood and George Clooney. Both have written, produced, directed and starred. Clint Eastwood won an Oscar for *Million Dollar Baby* (2005), which he directed and starred in and George Clooney for *Good Night and Good Luck* (2006) for supporting actor but which he co-wrote and directed.

The Oscars and star power

2006 was the 78th Annual Academy Awards. The first Oscar was awarded in 1928; it depicts a knight holding a crusader's sword, standing on a reel of film with five spokes signifying the original branches of the Academy: Actors, Writers, Directors, Producers and Technicians. Since this time the Awards have grown in both the size of the audience and in the fields of achievement covered. For example, in 1941, the documentary was added as a category, and in 2001, the first Animated Feature Oscar was awarded.

The Oscar for best actor in 2006 went to Philip Seymour Hoffman in his role as Truman Capote in the film *Capote* (Bennett Miller, Canada/USA, 2005). Hoffman is an interesting example of a character actor who has achieved stardom.

> Character actors seem to be a dying breed. It's testament to Philip Seymour Hoffman's versatility that he's held so many powerful roles and worked with the best writers and directors in modern cinema. Rather than settling into a stereotype or a character mould like the Pacinos and De Niros and Robin Williamses of the world, he's shrugged off each identity like a second skin and moved on to the next film …. For a stocky redhead with a devious looking face, he gets around. (www.acidlogic.com/im-hoffman.htm)

- You may like to discuss this quote with your students:
  - Do they agree that the actors named have slipped into character moulds?
  - Does success in one role mean you have to repeat it?
  - Are the roles they play variations on one character?
- How does an Academy Award change or improve a star's career? Ask your students to track two or three recent Oscar winners to see how this may have changed/improved the roles they had before. (They can do this on the website Oscars.com)

Hollywood since the 1950s

Information in this section is drawn from Richard Maltby's *Hollywood Cinema* (1995).

Following structural reorganisation in the 1950s, in the late 1960s Hollywood experienced further transformations as ownership of the industry's main production/distribution companies changed hands.

Conglomeration resulted from the acquisition of the former studios by other companies and corporate groups outside the film business. Paramount was acquired in 1966 by Gulf and Western, a large conglomerate with interests in manufacturing, agricultural products and financial services. As Gulf and Western increasingly concentrated its business around entertainment and publishing, the company was renamed Paramount Communications, Inc. It was subsequently sold in 1994 for $9.75 billion to Viacom, Inc. The sale of Paramount began an era in which the other major studios were bought by conglomerates. For example, Warner Bros. was sold in 1967 to the Canadian television distributor, Seven Arts, and was sold again two years later to a company, Warner Communications Inc., which sold off its other businesses to concentrate on entertainment. Coca-Cola acquired Columbia in 1982 and sold it in 1989 to the Sony Corporation.

With the wave of conglomeration came the trend towards diversification. The popular adoption of television in the 1950s had seen the Hollywood studios diversify into television production and distribution. Conglomeration combined the Hollywood studios with interests in other sectors of business, including the publishing, media and entertainment industries. When 20th Century-Fox was sold in 1985 it became part of the publishing and later television empire of News Corporation. In 1990, Warner Communications was sold to the powerful publisher Time, Inc., forming the largest entertainment company in the world.

● Production and marketing

Although ownership of the studios has changed, Hollywood continues to be based on the package-unit system of production. In the studio era films could be marketed in blocks with marketing costs spread across a number of films. However, in the package-unit system films are marketed individually with P and A (prints and advertising) expenditure attached to the single film. Figures indicate that equal emphasis is placed on the making and marketing of films in contemporary Hollywood.

During the 1990s the Motion Picture Association of America (MPAA), the industry body representing the collective interests of the major producers and distributors in Hollywood, estimated that for the films made by its members, the average production or negative cost (ie the cost of producing a feature film's finished negative) grew from $26.8 million in 1990 to $51.5 million in 1999. Marketing or prints and advertising costs grew in proportion from $12 million in 1990 to $24 million in 1999. The average cost of making and marketing features has nearly doubled from 1990 to 1999.

A useful resource on this topic is Justin Wyatt, *High Concept: Movies and Marketing in Hollywood* (1994).

Worksheet 7: Tracking a production asks students to look at an industry paper (*Screen International*), identify a film/project and build up a case study tracing the film's development over a period of time. They are asked to look at publicity materials, interviews etc, and to create a portfolio of information noting how the publicity intensifies as the release date approaches.

To access student worksheets and other online materials go to *Teaching Stars and Performance* at **www.bfi.org.uk/tfms** and enter User name: **stars@bfi.org.uk** and Password: **te1302sp**.

High-concept films

In the 1980s and 1990s films were increasingly to offer wider marketing opportunities. Market research informs not just the development of a successful film but also explores how the film may promote other merchandise, soundtracks, mugs etc. The term popularised in the industry in the 1980s for this kind of film was 'high concept'. A high-concept narrative is easy to market because the premise it is based on can be represented in a straightforward and uncomplicated manner. *Batman* (Tim Burton, USA, 1989) represented this trend.

Often the star is used as a means of illustrating the premise. According to this view the star becomes the premise and the premise is the thing that made the film and other products marketable eg, in *Top Gun* (Tony Scott, USA, 1986) the premise of the film could be summarised as 'fighter pilot in love'. The idea was marketed through the boyish good looks of Tom Cruise whose face appeared on the posters for the film and on the video for the song 'Take My Breath Away' by Berlin, a chart hit in North America and Europe. Cruise's image served to sell the film and attracted financing for the project through product placements for the sunglasses manufacturer Ray-Ban. Sales of leather jackets also apparently did well after the film, thus Cruise not only represented the film but also became a fashion role model.

At the end of the 1990s, films like *Con Air* (Simon West, USA, 1997), *Face/Off* (John Woo, USA, 1997), *Armageddon* (Michael Bay, USA, 1998) and *The Matrix* (Andy Wachowski and Larry Wachowski, USA, 1999) all provided examples of projects where star image and premise were closely intertwined to create a 'marketing event'.

Worksheet 8: High-concept products asks students to look at how a film is marketed to its maximum potential.

To access student worksheets and other online materials go to *Teaching Stars and Performance* at **www.bfi.org.uk/tfms** and enter User name: **stars@bfi.org.uk** and Password: **te1302sp**.

Stars and high-concept cinema

In the era of high-concept or event cinema, the value of stars as capital has increased. As negative costs rise, stars become even more central to the packaging of a project and the securing of production financing. Since the move to a package-unit system of production the powers of agents to act as key mediators in the industry have achieved new importance.

The package-unit system saw the agent begin to work at putting together script properties with directing and performing talent, taking a vital role in the development of projects which was formerly the responsibility of studio heads of production. MCA left the agency business in the 1960s but set an example for leading agencies in contemporary Hollywood. The William Morris Agency (WMA), Creative Artists Agency (CAA) and International Creative Management (ICM) are the three big agencies representing the majority of the stars in contemporary Hollywood.

Due to their central role in packaging projects, there is a tendency to assume that agencies have all the power but the studios still hold the money and agents are only powerful if they can place clients in packages which receive the backing of the studios.

While some stars still sign multi-package deals with a studio, it is more likely for agencies to negotiate for the use of a star's services on a film-by-film basis. Since James Stewart's contract with MCA, which included profit participation, stars' contracts now regularly include 'back-end' deals. Instead of taking a flat fee when a film is made, contractual agreements may see a star choosing to be paid based on a film's performance at the box office. The star is not fully remunerated at the time of production, but only when a film is distributed in all markets.

However, stars are not a pre-condition of profitability at the contemporary box office. Paul McDonald (2000) suggests that a list of the top films at the North American box office during the 1990s indicates a mixture of titles fronted by star names, together with equally successful films without stars at all. *Jurassic Park* (Steven Spielberg, USA, 1993) and *The Lost World: Jurassic Park* (Steven Spielberg, USA, 1997) featured well-known actors but no stars, *The Lion King* (Roger Allers, Rob Minkoff, USA, 1994), *Pocahontas* (Michael Gabriel and Eric Goldberg, USA, 1995), and the two *Toy Story* films (John Lasseter, USA, 1995 and 1999) may have used the voices of stars but these were not really utilised in their marketing. Dreamworks SKG, however, do use star names in their publicity campaigns. *Shrek*, *Shrek 2*, *A Shark Tale* and *Madagascar* made marketing use of the names of the stars voicing the characters.

The two articles which follow offer viewpoints and details about contemporary stars, their power and value in the context of production and marketing and how they influence the kind of films that are being made. Students are asked to examine the arguments and to consider the implications.

From 'The Trouble with Stars' by Peter Bart, editor-in-chief of *Variety*, and Peter Guber, studio chairman (*Guardian*, May 2003):

> … the star often receives a weekly non-accountable expense allowance of $15,000 per week. A jet aircraft could also be provided at a cost not to exceed $2,000 per hour for fuel and maintenance, plus $1,000 a day for two pilots and $250 a day for their accommodation. The star is also guaranteed a full-sized Mercedes Ben, a first-class trailer, two personal assistants, a separate make-up trailer, a dialogue coach, bodyguards, a personal chef, a personal trainer, plus free hotel rooms for visiting friends. The star is also given approval over the still photographer, plus wardrobe and make-up assistants and hair stylists. These kinds of deals often enable stars to earn more than the studio.

The movies need stars and the stars need movies, but to sustain the financial weight of star casting a film must be geared to the widest possible audience. It must offer a story accessible to the global market. The only way a superstar vehicle can justify its costs is if it's pre-designed to tap into all revenue streams, especially overseas television and video. Revenue from the US box office may constitute less than 30% of the overall totals.

The other article, 'The Star System Sucks', Fiachra Gibbons, *Guardian*, 14 May 2000, focuses on the stars themselves. Gibbons quotes Nick Nolte:

'The star system sucks, Hollywood has boiled itself down to four male leads and they have to be in all the big movies. ... The major studios pick the star first with no thought for material ...' (Nolte did not name Mel Gibson, Bruce Willis, Harrison Ford and George Clooney as the current Hollywood big 'four' but he doesn't have to.)

In **Worksheet 9: Stars today**, students are asked to list the points from two articles about the problems in making films in Hollywood today and to consider the implications.

1 of 3 pages

To access student worksheets and other online materials go to *Teaching Stars and Performance* at **www.bfi.org.uk/tfms** and enter User name: **stars@bfi.org.uk** and Password: **te1302sp**.

British cinema: Stars and Hollywood

The information and ideas in this section are drawn from Sara Street's *British National Cinema* (1997). She discusses the nature of stardom in Britain and how the influences of the theatrical tradition and the relationship with Hollywood have affected both audience and industry perceptions of stars. Discussions about British stardom have always been coloured by a patriotic ambivalence about aspiring to Hollywood models.

> Stardom … raises questions of national cinema cultures operating in a context of Hollywood domination but also within their own traditions and self-perception. The fact that for much of the century the British film industry has been in poor economic health has not prevented British stars from being important cultural icons in particular decades.

For a film industry that was formed mostly in the shadow of Hollywood, national stars provide an insight into the industry's self-perception in particular periods and reflect cultural assumptions about Britishness. Most of the top box-office stars in Britain were American, but the nation was not without its film stars and because of the British cinema's inferiority complex about Hollywood competition, home-grown stars were often invested with a patriotic imperative as bearers of British national culture.

> There has always been a tension between wanting British stars and all the trappings of gossip, fandom and scandal which are somehow unseemly, and 'unBritish'.

Britain's lack of a flourishing star system might also be partly because of links with the theatre where the pressures to behave as a star off stage do not exist in the same way that they do in film acting. Also, it seems that to win international fame British stars still need assistance from Hollywood in the form of roles or the accolade of Academy Awards – Kenneth Branagh, Daniel Day-Lewis, Anthony Hopkins, Miranda Richardson, Gary Oldman, Emma Thompson, Alan Rickman are all examples of this interaction with Hollywood. Other British stars who are big in Hollywood include Ewan McGregor, Michael Caine, Sean Connery, Kate Winslet, Keira Knightley, Clive Owen, Jude Law and Kate Beckinsale.

- Ask students to make a list of British and American stars and to compare their similarities and differences in terms of roles, publicity and audience perception.
- It might also be interesting to discuss what Renee Zellweger and Gwyneth Paltrow bring to British roles and British national identity through their star images.

● Cultural heritage

Critical discourse about what constitutes a good British film often dominates debates on British national cinema. In the 1930s, exploiting film's theatrical origins was considered to be an essential element in fostering British cinema, which could be identified by its specific cultural heritage. There was also an element of cultural snobbery about theatrical traditions exploited by film actors such as Jack Hawkins, John Gielgud, Michael Redgrave and Ralph Richardson who all considered their screen work to be secondary to their professional theatre work.

World War II was a significant period for film production in Britain, when Britain's literary and theatrical heritage was a source for scripts, which communicated particular ideas of the nation and Britishness. *Henry V* (Laurence Olivier, UK, 1944) and *This Happy Breed* (David Lean, UK, 1944), for example, transformed stage techniques into Technicolor film, demonstrating a sense of mission, confidence and prestige which characterised wartime British cinema. It established theatre actors, directors and writers, who contributed to the war effort on film. These included Sir Laurence Olivier, Ralph Richardson, Basil Dean and Terence Rattigan.

The Ministry of Information's task was to present the national point of view to the public at home and abroad. Lord Harold Macmillan (the first Minister of Information) stressed that in all propaganda there was to be an emphasis on British life and character showing the nation's 'independence, toughness of fibre, sympathy with the underdog ...' Many theatres were closed in the war and film offered actors stardom in the name of patriotism. This period was significant for the growth in the number of British stars such as James Mason, John Mills, Stewart Granger, Anna Neagle, Celia Johnson and Margaret Lockwood.

Worksheet 10: Britishness in conflict asks students to look at the kind of 'Britishness' that was emphasised in films produced during and after World War II, how much it conformed to the ideas proposed by the Ministry of Information and how these characteristics compare with British heroes portrayed in film today.

To access student worksheets and other online materials go to *Teaching Stars and Performance* at **www.bfi.org.uk/tfms** and enter User name: **stars@bfi.org.uk** and Password: **te1302sp**.

● Stereotypes

Most early film stars in Britain were already stars in the theatre and music hall. The economic problems of the British film industry in the 1920s made Hollywood an attractive place where many actors tried their luck on the screen. This exodus continued into the 1930s and included stars such as Errol Flynn, Herbert Marshall, George Sanders and Madeleine Carroll. Even though they no longer made films in Britain their work for Hollywood studios provided audiences with representations of Britishness in many top box-office films. Ronald Colman's image as the archetypical English gentleman was consolidated in many films including *Bulldog Drummond* (F Richard Jones, USA, 1929) and *The Prisoner of Zenda* (John Cromwell, USA, 1937). Many stereotypes of British behaviour originated in these Hollywood roles, producing constructions of Britishness from an American point of view. It is likely that these stereotypes, for example, the upper-class, laconic Englishman, influenced casting and characterisation in British films intended for the export market.

> The simple reference to the name of a popular star can summon up, evoke, a particular historical period: thus through their personae, stars come to stand as signifiers of the time in which they achieved their greatest popularity. (Sara Street, 1997)

● Students could research actors such as David Niven, Anna Neagle, Leslie Howard, Margaret Lockwood, Celia Johnson, Trevor Howard and discuss what characterises their film roles.

● The Rank Charm School

One institutional attempt from within the British film industry to present a conscious strategy of stardom was the Rank Charm School 1946–50. Gainsborough studios had tried to nurture a group of stars earlier in the 1940s but with Rank many British stars were actively involved in what amounted to a huge publicity campaign requiring them to behave like stars. They toured the country, attended beauty contests, film premieres and civic events and created an aura of British stardom which was popular with the public. It was important that stars were visible to the public and, by the 1940s, stardom was deeply embedded in popular cultural discourse. Dirk Bogarde and Diana Dors were two names associated with the School. The failure of the School could be seen as an indication of the British film industry's recurring and perpetual problems which were a result of not having large companies to promote stars for sustained periods, of not being able give them adequate screen exposure and of not possessing a sufficiently diverse industrial base to sustain a large number of independent companies.

Male stars and identity

In the 1950s, male stars such as Jack Hawkins, John Mills, Richard Todd, Dirk Bogarde and Norman Wisdom dominated British screens as opposed to the 1940s, which had been dominated by women (Margaret Lockwood, Anna Neagle, Phyllis Calvert). Female stars did not do so well at the box office and Britain did not appear to have the equivalent of a Marilyn Monroe or Kim Novak who could combine a desirable and glamorous physical appearance with a vulnerable innocence. Diana Dors came the closest to this. As for the representation of male sexuality in this period, popular male stars continued to portray conflicts over identity, particularly concerning issues of competence, assimilation into the family and class position.

These conflicts often involved the acceptance of duty and responsibility. Although Robert Murphy (1992) suggests that a wider range of acting talent came into the film industry in the 1960s – Albert Finney, Tom Courtenay, Rita Tushingham, Michael Caine, Sean Connery, Julie Christie – male characters continued to dominate as central protagonists and the main themes of 1960s' cinema were masculine problems.

● Focusing on male stars and identity is a useful way of looking at changes in British cinema over the decades. Examples include: *A Matter of Life and Death* (Michael Powell, Emeric Pressburger, UK, 1946), *Billy Liar* (John Schlesinger, UK, 1963), *Saturday Night and Sunday Morning* (Karel Reisz, UK, 1960), *A Room with a View* (James Ivory, UK, 1985), *Raining Stones* (Ken Loach, UK, 1993), *The Full Monty* (Peter Cattaneo, USA/UK, 1997) and the roles that Hugh Grant has played. They can examine issues within the films such as class, identity, masculinity and how the form/technical codes and genre of the films help to shape these identities.

● Directors and stars

Auteur theories and comparisons made between the British New Wave and the almost simultaneous French 'nouvelle vague' began to privilege directors above stars in terms of critical film discourse. The overall culture of expansion and experiment in the 1960s encouraged actors to become directors and producers. For example, Bryan Forbes, Richard Attenborough and Jack Hawkins formed Allied Film Makers in 1959, and Albert Finney directed himself in *Charlie Bubbles* (UK, 1967).

This creative decade of filmmaking was curtailed when a large number of American-backed films failed at the box office towards the end of the 1960s and cinema admissions plummeted from 327 million in 1965 to 193 million in 1970. British output and investment in 1973 had fallen by half compared with 1972 and this had serious implications for film stars.

After American companies pulled out of financing British films in the 1970s, the fragmented nature of the British film industry created difficulties for actors seeking to establish a star image. The exploitation of stars requires a fairly stable economic base so actors could not become stars within the British film industry. Sean Connery as James Bond was a star partly because United Artists financed so many Bond pictures, creating a familiar body of work, knowledge of which audiences could bring with them when viewing each new Bond film. Connery worked with a range of directors in Britain and Hollywood, while Michael Caine left Britain in 1978 and went on to international stardom in Hollywood films while Albert Finney and Tom Courtenay returned to the theatre.

Nevertheless, as far as popular cinema in the 1960s was concerned star names were big box office, and the New Wave dramas were by no means the most popular films. Aspects of conventional fandom and star culture were becoming more fragmented with the rise of pop music and television. *Picturegoer*, the major British fan magazine since the 1930s, folded in 1958 and its final issues revealed how pop culture was invading film fandom. Richard Lester's *A Hard Day's Night* (UK, 1964) has four male stars, the Beatles, at the centre of its narrative and their new kind of celebrity is the main theme of the film. The Beatles are an example of the traditional attributes of film stardom being extended to a very wide audience at the time when mass popular culture meant new young audiences. Like other stars they were both ordinary and extraordinary, their unattainability being a major focus of attraction for their girl fans.

Worksheet 11: Contemporary British stars asks students to read a summary of Danny Leigh's article, 'Usual Suspects' (*Guardian*, 30 August 2002, at www.guardianunlimited.com) and consider the arguments about contemporary British and American stars. They are then invited to prepare two star case studies considering career, roles and publicity – one American and one British.

1 of 2 pages

To access student worksheets and other online materials go to *Teaching Stars and Performance* at **www.bfi.org.uk/tfms** and enter User name: **stars@bfi.org.uk** and Password: **te1302sp**.

● An aristocratic tradition?

Julian Petley suggests that most British stars of the 1970s and 1980s were too stage-bound in technique and vision. He comments on the success of Jeremy Irons:

> To date his success as a star is principally founded on his impersonation of a familiar English stereotype: a pre-World War II English gentleman, slightly decadent preferably with an ambiguous sexual identity. The fact that Rupert Everett has been so sensationally successful in just such a role in *Another Country* … suggests not so much the need for an English pin-up equivalent of Richard Gere but rather the potent appeal of this particular stereotype at the present moment, relating as it does to such familiar English vices as nostalgia for the imperial past, an obsession with failure and humiliation and a highly ambiguous fascination with the mores (especially sexual) of the upper classes (cited by Street, 1997).

Street argues that this description places Jeremy Irons in the established tradition of British actors, including David Niven, Michael Wilding, Kenneth More, James Fox and other such upper-class English types and anticipates the aristocratic Hugh Grant with his very similar star persona in *Four Weddings and a Funeral* (Mike Newell, 1994). This particular representation has won consistent favour in America.

> Hugh Grant is an interesting example of an upper class star whose career has been curiously assisted by his arrest in Los Angeles in 1995 with a prostitute. His persona is that of the well-bred Englishman whose off-screen behaviour merely confirms stereotypes about upper-class hypocrisy over sexual matters. Although international success has made him a star, he nevertheless comes across in interviews as a modest, stuttering, even bashful man. In turn, this behaviour has encouraged his fans to interpret 'the Divine incident' as an endearing schoolboy misdemeanour. (Sara Street, 1997)

In some ways the scandal of the Divine Brown incident (Hugh Grant was arrested in America for being caught in a compromising situation with a prostitute) enhanced his star image and allowed him to play bad boy roles. Other scandals have not always had such positive effect: Fatty Arbuckle, a comic actor, was acquitted of rape and murder in San Francisco in 1921. Paramount, however, cancelled his contract and he never acted again. It has been suggested that Russell Crowe's phone throwing scandal had a negative effect on the box-office takings for *Cinderella Man* (Ron Howard, USA, 2005). In Case study 2, students are asked to consider Hugh Grant's screen image and his star persona and discuss his contribution to the success of Working Title films in Britain and abroad.

Critical approaches

The information in this section has been drawn from *Approaches to Popular Film* by Joanne Hollows and Mark Jancovich (1995), *Stars* by Richard Dyer (1998) and Paul McDonald's chapter on 'Star Studies' in the same book.

● The semiotic approach

Paul McDonald refers to Richard Dyer's work on stars (*Stars*, 1979 and *Heavenly Bodies*, 1987) in which he suggests that stars can be perceived as texts whose images are formed out of a series of signs which carry particular ideological meanings: a star is a product of the particular meanings that that star signifies.

This semiotic approach allows us to:

- Study the differences between stars through an analysis of the precise signs deployed in their star images;
- See that the appeal of stars is not the product of some unique, magical quality inherent in the individual star but of the ways in which a star works in relation to certain ideological issues such as class, gender or race;
- See that stars can be viewed not simply as part of industry manipulation, but as a product of certain constructions of cultural identity (not purely individual tastes).

Dyer suggests that the appeal of stars lies in the way in which their image can resolve ideological contradictions for the audience. For example, Marilyn Monroe resolved certain contradictory notions of femininity and female sexuality, particularly the meanings of sexiness and innocence. However, while he argued that the star's image was a construct, not a pure expression of their real personality, he also pointed out that the signs which construct this image are still deployed by someone – the actual performer. It is part of the way in which stars act to resolve ideological contradictions. The star's image resolves its contradictory elements partly because they are signified as the property of one person. These meanings become attached to that person and naturalised as though part of the star's individual identity.

Julia Roberts

In 1991 Richard Dyer offered an analysis of Julia Roberts as a star. He suggested 1991 was the year of Julia Roberts and introduced the idea of the 'star moment' – a moment when the particular meanings signified by the persona or image of the star coincided in some way with the contemporary attitudes, values or ideologies which seemed important in society.

According to him, Roberts combined the following oppositions:

sex object	in charge of own image
vulnerable	no pushover
playing with image	authenticity
consumerism	caring attitudes

bimbo ←————————————→ housewife

By embodying these different values and qualities, Julia Roberts, as star, brought them into play as part of the dramatic structure of her films during the late 1980s and early 1990s. In representing such opposites, the star seemed able to steer a course between them and offered a synthesis of things an audience finds difficult or impossible to bring together in daily life. She became a fantasy role model and a fantasy figure of desire.

The star image is more than just a visual one. The persona (the mix of real person and character role) must also engage interest and produce meaning. In modern stars like Julia Roberts this is often focused on the idea of 'authenticity' encouraging a link between the real person and the character in the mind of the spectator. Media stories about Julia Roberts and her relationship with her male leads conveyed the idea that she was just 'being herself'. The characters she played at this time demonstrated a mixture of strength and vulnerability, suggesting an embodiment of those roles by Roberts the real person. The spectator is presented with the paradox of stardom – the star seems knowable and accessible, and, at the same time, extraordinary and only attainable in a spectator's fantasy.

Other semiotic concepts

Maximised types: Individualism is a central value in American society and this more general ideological meaning is contained in all Hollywood stars. The star can be a 'maximised type' – as perfect an embodiment of a set of characteristics as can be imagined. This allows the culture to perpetuate its myths, whether they are of masculine heroism, female beauty or self-actualisation through lifestyle. In the development of a unique, individualised identity through image, the ideological reinforcement provided by the star is very powerful.

Star as signifier: Saussure proposes that the sign can be divided into the 'signifier' (the material component such as the markings that make up the written word) and the 'signified' (the concept which is associated with those markings). Barthes argues that while a particular signifier will denote particular meaning, there will be further meanings which are connoted by that sign. For example, a photograph (signifier) of Arnold Schwarzenegger (signified) connotes further meanings such as masculinity and Americanness. This idea operates not just within the textual space of a genre-based, narrative realist film. The star also exists in the broader culture and in this existence can have more diverse meanings. Madonna, for example, highlights and negotiates contradictions about gender and sexuality.

Star as structure: The star's presence is likely to be made up of recurring features which lead to a high degree of predictability and associated audience expectations. The star contains qualities, characteristics and meanings which generate repetition and variety from one film to another. Meanings become attached to that person and naturalised – they appear to be a natural and inherent aspect of the star's individual identity rather than socially constructed.

- Show students half a dozen pictures of contemporary stars and ask them to call out the meanings that they associate with them. Explore how they may differentiate the 'meanings' of, for example, Bruce Willis from Leonardo DiCaprio, Robert de Niro from Samuel Jackson or Keira Knightley from Cameron Diaz.
- Introduce a synopsis of a contemporary Hollywood film and discuss how the meaning of the film might change with different stars in the main role. For example, Robert de Niro in *Blade Runner* (Ridley Scott, USA, 1982), Johnny Depp in *Fight Club* (David Fincher, Germany/USA, 1999), Denzel Washington in *Gladiator* (Ridley Scott, USA, 2000).

Worksheet 12: Stars and their meanings invites students to investigate Richard Dyer's ideas and explain oppositional meanings contained in contemporary stars.

To access student worksheets and other online materials go to *Teaching Stars and Performance* at **www.bfi.org.uk/tfms** and enter User name: **stars@bfi.org.uk** and Password: **te1302sp**.

● The intertextual approach

Star images are the product of intertextuality in which the non-filmic texts of promotion, publicity and criticism interact with the film text. Although the star's name and body anchor the image to one person, the process of intertextual associations is so complex that the meaning of a star's image is never limited, stable or total. This intertextuality is not simply an extension of the star's meaning but is the only meaning that the star ever has – the star's image does not exist outside this shifting series of texts.

Historical context: The intertextual approach is valuable in that it enables us to reconstruct the meanings which specific stars acquire at specific historical moments. In his study of Monroe, Richard Dyer examines ways in which Monroe's star image served to redefine female sexuality in 1950s' America. Dyer reads across a series of texts from the period (for example, *Playboy* and *Reader's Digest*) to establish the discourse of femininity which was prevalent in the period. Monroe's public and private image 'conforms to, and is part of the construction of, what constitutes desirability in women.' Her blondeness and vulnerability offered a construction of female sexuality which is unthreatening and willing.

Private and public: In Western societies, the separation of public and private spheres has resulted in a preoccupation with identifying the truth of ourselves, a truth which is supposedly hidden behind appearances. It is possible to understand that stars fascinate because their performances make the private self into a public spectacle, as they seem to reveal the truths of their selves within a public forum.

Worksheet 13: Stars and intertextuality asks students to investigate two stars from different historical periods, looking at how a range of texts contribute to and reinforce the meaning of that particular star at that particular time.

To access student worksheets and other online materials go to *Teaching Stars and Performance* at **www.bfi.org.uk/tfms** and enter User name: **stars@bfi.org.uk** and Password: **te1302sp**.

● Stars and spectators

Both the semiotic and intertextual approaches to star images clearly imply that there is a spectator or audience. Paul McDonald cites John Ellis who, like Richard Dyer, regards stars as intertextual constructions, but distinguishes between the primacy of the film performance and the subsidiary texts of journalism and gossip. For the spectator, the star image emerges from the fragments of subsidiary texts, but it does so as an 'incomplete image' which is only completed in the film performance – audiences are motivated to go to see stars by the desire to complete the puzzle of the star's image.

Psychoanalytical criticism regards the act of viewing film as fundamentally bound up with issues of desire related to the figure of the star.

- *The look*: The film text is organised around three types of looks: the spectator who looks at the screen; the camera which 'looks at the action'; and the characters in the film who look at one another. These looks create the conditions within which the spectator relates to stars, particularly through a process of identification.
- *The mirror stage*: According to Lacan, children go through the mirror stage between six and 18 months: they identify with an image of the independent self, which is perceived through a mirror. The mirror image appears complete and masterful, in contrast to the powerlessness of their actual body, and is the object of narcissistic identification. It is argued that cinema echoes this moment of the child's development, but substitutes the screen for the mirror. It replays the narcissistic process of identification. The audience identifies with the stars, who appear to them as complete in their construction; stars become idealised selves for the audience.
- *The spectator as voyeur*: The star is also presented as an object to be gazed at by the spectator voyeuristically. Unlike the theatre, where the spectator and performer are in the same room, cinema separates the spectator and the star in time and space. The star is absent although the cinematic image gives the impression of presence.

● Feminist film theory

Feminist approaches to film criticism are primarily concerned with analysing Hollywood's construction of women. They mainly assume this dominant cinema is grounded in patriarchy: representing woman according to the dominant ideologies of gender in society and using cinema to reinforce dominant ideologies of femininity. Classical Hollywood represents women, according to these views, as essentially passive stereotypes (madonna/whore, wife/mistress, good mother/bad mother).

Laura Mulvey's article 'Visual Pleasure and Narrative Cinema', which appeared in *Screen* in 1975, investigated the pleasure of looking. She asserted that mainstream cinema organises the spectator in a gender-specific way by suggesting that Hollywood cinematic practice had established a code of spectatorship where women were presented as sexual spectacle both as objects of pleasure for the characters within the narrative and for the spectator in the auditorium. She drew on psychoanalysis to work out the inequalities of the gaze and in psychoanalytic terms she argued that men could not look at women as equals because this would castrate them. To avoid this castration, men fetishise women, imbuing them with an overvalued and unrealistic status. She termed this 'fetishistic scopophilia'.

This analysis highlighted the sexist practices of Hollywood and drew attention to the ways in which women were objectified by the cinema. However, part of Laura Mulvey's project in writing this piece was to 'destroy pleasure'. The submission to pleasure was seen as central in supporting the subjugation of women propagated by cinematic practice.

She argued that in cinema, pleasure is related to issues of sexual difference and sexual politics. The spectator's look, and that of the camera, are both mediated by the ways in which male characters look at female characters. The male star acts as the spectator's ideal self. He is a point of identification rather than an object of desire. The female star is defined as the object of his gaze. She is defined as a passive sexual spectacle. The subject of that look is defined as male and the woman is defined as the object of that look. Cinema centres pleasure in male heterosexual desire, and defines the female as the passive object of male desire.

The 'gaze' was constructed in these ways:

- By the cameraman and production team in the establishment and framing of a shot;
- By the look within the film: male characters objectify female ones through their active, desiring and powerful 'look';
- By the way the spectator's gaze is constructed through the above mechanisms.

More recent psychoanalytic film theory has seen a move away from the assumption that the spectator only identifies with a single narrative figure and towards the claim that he or she engages in a more complex identification with the overall narrative. Any narrative provides that spectator with multiple and shifting points of identification.

Many critics have criticised Mulvey's tendency to neglect the pleasures of female spectatorship. Her theory only allows women to either identify with the male protagonist or else identify with the position of passive sex object. Accordingly she ruled out any prospect of a female gaze from the analysis. She argued that for women to enjoy the images of pleasure they must be either acting as 'honorary men' or be 'masochistic'. However, Hollywood's history has constantly demonstrated the deification of male stars by female audiences, such as Rudolph Valentino, Clark Gable and Brad Pitt.

● Films which could illustrate Laura Mulvey's theories are *Peeping Tom* (Michael Powell, UK, 1960) and *Halloween* (John Carpenter, USA, 1978) (opening sequences) where the camera's point of view is that of the male predator. Other films which will promote discussion are *Legends of the Fall* (Edward Zwick, USA, 1994) where the audience is invited to admire Brad Pitt's beauty (a male star) and *Thelma and Louise* (Ridley Scott, USA, 1991) in the sequence where they rob the store. (This sequence is very much about 'looking'; the detectives and Thelma's husband are watching their activities through CCTV footage and are powerless to act.) *The Blair Witch Project* (Daniel Myrick, Eduardo Sánchez, USA, 1999) also offers an interesting sequence where the 'heroine' films herself speaking to her own camera, filming herself.

Debating 'the gaze'

Mulvey's work triggered a debate among feminist film scholars about the issue of looking. Mary Ann Doane continued the argument and suggested that the gaze itself is 'gendered'. She contended that for women to gaze at men was to merely reinforce the view that the system of looking was dependent upon aligning sexual difference with a subject/object dichotomy. She went on to suggest that the male and female gaze could never be equal and argued that women have only a 'marginal' gaze while men possess a 'centred' one. The difficulty that women have with looking comes from the position they find themselves in society, ie marginal figures in a central patriarchy. She also discusses 'foregrounding the masquerade', which is the deliberate flaunting of female sexuality in order to disrupt the power relationship established by the male gaze: attempting to control the male gaze by deliberate exploitation of it. She suggests that femininity is a performance which is socially constructed rather than natural and inherent. In a similar way, the hyper-masculine bodies of Schwarzenegger and Stallone flaunt a performance of masculinity and so reveal masculinity to be a sign, not an innate property of being male. Star performances and gender performances are social constructions.

Susan Faludi, in her 'Backlash' theory, discusses a series of Hollywood films in the late 1980s and 1990s featuring very negative representations of career women, suggesting that *Fatal Attraction* (Adrian Lyne, USA, 1987), *Basic Instinct* (Paul Verhoeven, USA, 1992) and *The Hand That Rocks the Cradle* (Curtis Hanson, USA, 1992) were a backlash against the successes that women had during that period in terms of careers and salary.

Annette Kuhn argues that

The industry wants to let everyone have their ideological cake and eat it too. In other words, you'll see deliberate ambiguities structured into every film to come out about strong women. (1999)

Suzanne Moore (1988) attributes the elevation of stars like Schwarzenegger and Stallone to a shift in political renegotiation over masculinity brought about over the last 20 years. She suggests that change has taken place at the economic base, which influences changes in the ideological structure. Society is thus changing the way it thinks about masculinity: there is a more active female gaze and there is a growing male narcissism.

Some theorists argue that the male body on display is not under the same viewing conditions as the female body (Van Zoonen, 1994). While texts might show some shifts in representation, it is not as a result of shifts in power at the site of production, but a result of commercial imperatives. In terms of media production, things have to make commercial sense. If money can be made, an active female gaze is recruited in a text, for example, in the proliferation of boy bands in popular music and the male striptease. The overwhelming reality is that 'the dominant visual economy is still organised along traditional gender lines: men look at women, women watch themselves being looked at.' (Kuhn, 1999)

Worksheet 14: Looking at stars asks students to collect examples of what they consider to be the male and female gaze in advertising, on websites, and in film and television and to discuss examples which seem ambivalent.

To access student worksheets and other online materials go to *Teaching Stars and Performance* at **www.bfi.org.uk/tfms** and enter User name: **stars@bfi.org.uk** and Password: **te1302sp.**

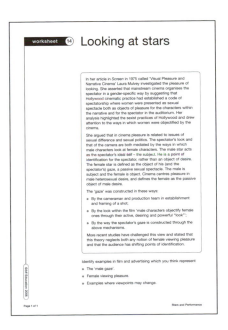

● Stars and audiences

Stars attract audiences and thus add:

- Insurance value by guaranteeing the success of a film project. Whether in the studio system under lengthy contract or in the new Hollywood as part of a 'package', stars are major attractions for film audiences.
- Production value by bringing something unique to the film, based on the star's persona and image, which can be exploited to enhance the overall meaning and effect of the film. To measure what a star brings to a film, try substituting one star for another in a specific film role.
- Trademark value by combining elements of the previous two values to contribute a set of characteristics that can be mobilised for publicity and marketing purposes. It is more than just a sign of quality – like a guarantee – it is also a condensed meaning, a communication of what the film will be about and what kind of viewing experience it promises.

Studying audiences

Moviegoers can be categorised according to class, gender, sexuality, race, nation and age.

Each of these categories affects the understanding and the appeal of a star for each individual moviegoer. Audiences make sense of stars within social and historical contexts – they are not closed texts.

For example, Jackie Stacey studied women's responses to Hollywood stars of the 1940s and 1950s. Her respondents revealed a variety of types of identification. Her analysis reveals the following categories:

- 'Devotion, adoration and worship', in which women moviegoers praise a star's difference from themselves.
- 'Transcendence' where a moviegoer wishes to overcome the difference between herself and the star so that she can become more like the star.
- 'Aspiration' and 'inspiration' where the moviegoer values the personality and behaviour of the star, and sees the star's power and confidence as providing her with a positive role model.

A spectator gets pleasure from identifying with a star, both passively and actively by:

- Pretending (the spectator acts out the fantasy of being the star knowing that the act is make-believe).
- Resembling (the spectator has an actual physical similarity to the star and may selectively emphasise it to become associated with the star's image).
- Imitating behaviour (the spectator's similarity is not actual but acquired).
- Copying of appearance rather than aspects of behaviour.

Performance

In *Hollywood Cinema* (1995), Richard Maltby offers a detailed background to performance in Hollywood, from which this summary is taken.

● Constructing meaning in film

In the early 1920s, Lev Kuleshov may have edited together a sequence of shots that has since become one of the most discussed pieces of lost film in cinema history. According to Kuleshov's pupil, Vesvolod Pudovkin, he cut together a close-up of the actor Ivan Mosjoukineì's expressionless face with three other shots – a bowl of soup, a child playing with a toy bear and a woman lying in a coffin. The shot of the actor's face was the same in all three shots, but the audience praised his acting and commented on the sorrow with which he looked at the coffin, the happy smile when he surveyed the child at play and the pensiveness of his mood when he looked at the forgotten soup. Although the footage has been lost, this experiment has contributed to theories of how cinema and cinema acting constructs meaning. The results of the experiment were also fundamental to the montage-based approach of Soviet cinema.

Pudovkin's argument was that 'film is not shot but built, built up from the separate strips of celluloid that are its raw material'. He maintained that the juxtaposition of the close-up of the actor and each of the other shots generated a precise and predictable meaning in the mind of the spectator that was not actually present in the shots alone. Spectators, however, understood the meaning to be the result of the actor's performance: a performance apparently created by editing.

The resulting theory of the production of cinematic meaning corresponded to both ideological and aesthetic preferences of early Soviet society – the juxtaposition of two shots, thesis and antithesis, produced the synthesis of the spectator's recognition of sorrow or happiness. Pudovkin's theory of montage emphasised the power of the cinematic machine, under the control of the director and editor to create meaning with the reliability of a factory assembly line: 'the camera compels the spectator to see as the director wishes but it was the task of the director to direct the spectator's attention'.

Maltby comments that whatever the reliability of the accounts of the Kuleshov experiment, they do suggest the extent to which a cinematic performance is never constructed by an actor alone. Cinematic acting differs most obviously from theatrical acting in the way that a cinematic performance is discontinuous, fragmented into the individual shots which are the movie's constituent parts before being reassembled in the editing room. The constructed nature of a movie emphasises the extent to which a movie performance is not only the work of the actor. Several different bodies may be used to construct a single performance: voices are dubbed, stunt artists are used for dangerous action sequences, and sometimes hand models and body doubles provide body parts to substitute for the actors. A movie is also constructed out of the performance of the camera, the editing and the *mise en scène*.

● Physical movement and narrative

The word 'cinema' is derived from the Greek word for motion, *kinema*, but the extent to which movement is emphasised by different filmmakers varies. Hollywood gives movement a much higher status than European cinema and calls its products moving pictures rather than films. As well as offering spectacular interludes, physical movement within the frame is a principal source of story information and the basis of many of our perceptions about characters.

Movement can mean the movement of objects within the frame, the movement of the camera itself and the movement produced in the editing process. Maltby offers *Bullitt* (Peter Yates, USA, 1968) as an example of a film which combines these three types of movement with the car chase, viewpoint shots and panning shots. The sequence, as a whole, emphasises the impression of speed for its own sake, rather than developing the narrative possibilities of the scene. Nearly all Hollywood films have at least one sequence which displays action or physical expertise, interrupting the narrative and challenging its dominance. Musical sequences are good examples of this shift between motivations. *Singin' in the Rain* is an example of how performances take place outside the narrative constraints of the movie

- Ask students to provide examples of movement in contemporary film which interrupt and/or halt the narrative. These can be action sequences or song-and-dance numbers.

● Performance style

Hollywood appropriates performance styles from a variety of theatrical traditions (vaudeville, circus, pantomime and burlesque) and from radio and television. In part, this simply follows the industrial practice of exploiting talent already trained in other theatrical disciplines; in part, it suggests that different performance styles are necessary in different genre contexts. The relative cultural status of Hollywood movies is largely governed by the kind of performance they sponsor – some of Hollywood's most respectable movies (for example, *Who's Afraid of Virginia Woolf?*, USA, Mike Nichols, 1966) have been versions of critically acclaimed stage plays, while few physical comedies, musicals or action adventures have won Academy Awards for Best Picture or

Best Performance. Maltby comments that the higher status of acting is in part derived from the cultural prestige of straight theatre in comparison to vaudeville, and in part from its aspirations to 'truth' or verisimilitude in the imitation of character.

Acting in Hollywood films aspires toward transparency in the same way that codes of editing and camerawork seek to make themselves invisible. This 'invisible' style of acting tries to imitate the expressions and emotions of the everyday world; its aim is to create a sense of character for the audience without making them consciously aware of how that sense is created. Characters need convincing motives for their actions, and these are most readily supplied by patterns of behaviour and psychology that we recognise from our everyday world. Frank McConnell sees film acting as being radically different from theatre acting in terms of the actor's relation to space and the audience. The craft of the stage actor is to assimilate himself or herself to a predetermined role that becomes realised in his or her physical presence on the stage for the audience which is there is front of him or her, but the film actor never shares a common space with the audience and the dynamics of the relationship are different. The stage actor has to persuade the audience to 'see through' his or her presence to the character. The film actor has first of all to assert his or her own physical presence against the artifice and mechanisms of cinema's capacity to fragment and deconstruct time, place and the body.

In *Acting in the Cinema*, James Naremore (1988) makes a distinction between presentational and representational modes of acting. Presentational styles acknowledge the co-presence of performer and audience, usually through a conventionalised form of direct address such as a Shakespearean aside. Representational styles offer the audience the illusion that the performers – or the cinematic apparatus that records the action – are invisible to the audience.

It is often suggested that the studio system restricted star performers by typecasting them into roles, restricting the range of their acting and leading to charges that many stars, such as John Wayne, could not act as they always 'played themselves'. This may be an expression of the perceived low cultural status of films.

Maltby also suggests that in America, the actor and not the text is the most important element in a play or a film. The star is present as a production value and as a known bundle of personality traits and performs his or her star persona in a movie. At the same time the star as an actor is 'disappearing' into his or her role. There is a paradoxical element in the idea of the actor's disappearance. In every performance two identities – actor and character – inhabit the same body, and in the naturalistic style of acting (called invisible) the skill of the actor consists in eliding the difference between the two identities, in disembodying himself or herself to embody the role. The 'invisible' technical skill is, paradoxically, most apparent when the character is physically different from the actor: Dustin Hoffman's performances as a woman in *Tootsie* (Sydney Pollack, USA, 1982) and the autistic Raymond in *Rain Man* (Barry Levinson, USA, 1988) are examples of this.

● Ask students to provide a range of examples of actors who 'disappear' into their roles and others who offer some variety on a recognisable character.

● The person and the star

The emphasis on the person of the actor is most explicit in star performances. The commercial imperative of the star system requires that stars, like Clint Eastwood, Sylvester Stallone, Jack Nicholson, or Marilyn Monroe, are always visible through their characters. An established star is, literally, a body of expectations and these bodies function as economic narrative devices. A great deal of information is conveyed about characters simply because they are played by a star such as Clark Gable or Bette Davis.

Worksheet 15: Expectations and narrative devices explores audience expectations and stars as narrative devices.

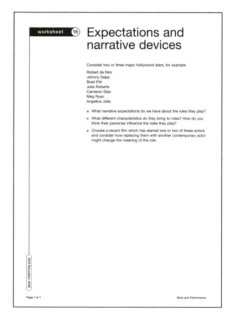

To access student worksheets and other online materials go to *Teaching Stars and Performance* at **www.bfi.org.uk/tfms** and enter User name: **stars@bfi.org.uk** and Password: **te1302sp**.

Classical Hollywood's star system constructed a correspondence between star and role that was embodied in Clark Gable's casting as Rhett Butler in *Gone with the Wind*. The common recognition that a role might have been written for a particular actor did no more than acknowledge the actualities of Hollywood industrial practice, by which scripts were written specifically to exhibit the already established traits and mannerisms of their stars. The fact that a star's persona circulated in the media in the promotion of specific films allowed for a considerable interaction between the star's performance and off-screen persona. This created persona was often seen as sufficient and satisfying for an audience and there was no need to offer a variety of roles.

Many star careers have been constructed around the play of variation centred on a star's public persona. In Marilyn Monroe's case, the play lay in the combination of an innocence expressed by her voice and gestures and sexual promise expressed by her body, making her sexually alluring and vulnerable at the same time and allowing for a constant play between aspects of her fictional character and her off-screen persona, for example, *Gentlemen Prefer Blondes* (Howard Hawks, USA, 1953) and *Some Like It Hot*.

In the production of a star vehicle the character is often adapted to the star. This centres the plot on a character who eventually displays the skills that the audience knows the performer possesses. In Bette Davis's case, once her persona had been firmly fixed in the public imagination, it opened up opportunities for off-casting in roles that opposed her established image (the villainess). The marketing logic of this was that she was contracted to appear in three movies a year and audiences might tire of seeing three similar performances.

With off-casting filmmakers can invoke audience expectations while offering something new, an example being Tom Cruise's performance in *Collateral* (Michael Mann, USA, 2004). Such negotiations are the common currency in which the star system conveys information through convention and audience expectation rather than through a more realist characterisation. Criticisms of typecasting misunderstand the industrial function of the star performance, where the audience must first recognise Clark Gable as Clark Gable and then transform their engagement with his presence into an investment in the character he plays and the story being told.

Worksheet 16: Performance and the body offers students a range of statements about performance and asks them to consider them in the light of certain film texts, such as *Broken Blossoms* (D W Griffith, USA, 1919), *Angels with Dirty Faces* (Michael Curtiz, USA, 1938) and *Secrets and Lies* (Mike Leigh, UK, 1996).

Performance and gesture

In her article 'Putting on a Show, or the Ghostliness of Gesture', Lesley Stern makes interesting points on performance and gesture in cinema by considering a particular film genre – the film about the show (www.sensesofcinema.com/contents/02/21sd_s).

Lesley Stern explains how performance is not limited just to the actor's performance but encompasses a larger frame that includes the interaction of various cinematic codes and processes – acting techniques and cinematic technologies. However, the body of the actor – its disposition, movement and timing – is crucial, and the 'gestural' is always important in 'fleshing out' the diegetic world (the world of the film itself). It is the actor's body which is at the same time fictional and indexical of the real that provides a vital link between the movies and the world we, the audience, inhabit outside the cinema.

Gesture and its reappearance and repetition in cinema provides evidence not just of one particular figure or one particular passion – but evokes more generally a recognisable performative register. In other words, a gesture which belongs to a group of gestures is instantly recognised and given meaning to by audiences. It does this by reanimating an archaic sign, a sign of gestural theatricality, for example, 'the diva gesture', with both arms raised above head, a gesture which resonates from silent film to the present day. (Gestures are not necessarily specific to cinema – they might migrate from one movie to another, from films into social contexts and vice versa. They resonate, disappear and reappear differently and the differences may depend on the cultural and historical context as well as the medium and genre.)

Gestures are performed individually but they are not possessed by, nor are they particular to, individuals. They acquire force and significance through repetition and variation. They are never simply signs but indicate relationships, imagined as well as real, between films and audiences, stars and fans, characters and actors.

● Before looking at particular examples, ask students to brainstorm recognisable gestures which carry the same meaning from film to film, such as the connotations of 'the high five', or gestures associated with particular actors, such as Robert de Niro, Cameron Diaz, Jim Carrey, Ben Stiller, Jennifer Aniston.

Performance cannot be isolated – it is brought to life through a relationship with an audience. Performance studies tell us that the performance text includes both performers and audience – the transfer of energy, the process of reading. In the theatre the emphasis is on the 'aliveness' of the space and time that includes both performers and audience. Film Studies does pay attention to the process of viewing and to the realm of the visual but also to the idea that to be part of an audience is not merely to see but also to feel, to experience a range of somatic (bodily) responses.

'Putting on a show' films

The films which Lesley Stern uses to illustrate her points take as their subject matter the theatre, showbiz or television and include: *42nd Street* (Lloyd Bacon, USA, 1933) and *The Band Wagon* (Vincente Minnelli, USA, 1953); *The King of Comedy* (Martin Scorsese, USA, 1983) and *Bamboozled* (Spike Lee, USA, 2000); and *All About Eve* (Joseph L Mankiewicz, USA, 1950) and *Opening Night* (John Cassavetes, USA, 1977).

She suggests that all six films have similar patterns and variations and to understand these patterns she proposes four analytical categories: – generic tropes, thematic motifs, figurative formations and performative modalities.

- **Generic tropes** are privileged moments, hyphenated scenarios, dramatic dynamics which, although embedded in the narrative, have a certain recognisable autonomy as 'set-pieces', their function is rhetorical and generic rather than connected to the narrative eg, the big break, the audition, the rehearsal, the opening night …

- **Thematic motifs** are grounded in the diegesis (the world of the film) and they include high culture versus low culture, theatre versus film, disaster versus success, public versus private.

- **Figurative formations** refer on the one hand to the range of stock figures – star celebrity, producer/director, ingénue, understudy, ghost, diva and, on the other hand, to the varying range of relations that this 'cast' enables, and to the emotional tenor of these relations: admiration, love, erotic energy, emulation, envy, revenge.

- **Performative modalities.** These are all cast in a dialectical (oppositional) form, including: histrionic/quotidian (everyday), inflation/deflation, the daily body/the extra-daily body; on stage/off stage; on-screen/ off-screen acting, actor/role, stage/screen which lead onto theatre/films, self/other, performer/audience. This final dialectic or opposition – performer/audience (viewer) – turns out to be the most fundamental modality in the performance text. What these films 'stage' is a nuanced and multiple viewing place and also a sensory expansion, so that to be an audience is not merely to see but also to feel, to experience a range of physical (or bodily) responses.

42nd Street

At the audition in *42nd Street*, the hopefuls line up on the stage, which is contained in the film frame, and we, the film viewers, are positioned as part of the theatre audience (this can be called intradiegetic as it blends two worlds – that of the film and that of the audience). It is a musical and a backstage drama – and introduces many of the 'putting on a show' features: the ingénue, the big break, an onstage/offstage and audience/performer dialectic and the stage/screen dynamic. There are variations in point of view throughout the film but on the whole the film respects the theatrical stage as the place of performance as the narrative moves from audition to rehearsal to the anticipation of the opening night. The diva twists her ankle and the ingénue gets her big break, her man and stardom.

The film concludes with the opening night of the show but, choreographed by Busby Berkeley, this is a cinematic spectacle. The camera abandons the stage audience's point of view and the cinematic apparatus acts as part of a kaleidoscopic moving picture to produce a visual feast with an exhilarating, kinaesthetic effect. This conjunction of cinematic technology and performing bodies offers us not the opening night of a stage show but a cinematic performance. The dancing bodies are important while the individual star decreases in importance.

The Band Wagon

Twenty years later in *The Band Wagon*, Vincente Minnelli uses what by now was a well-established subgenre, the backstage drama, to make a highly reflexive film about musicals. Much of the pleasure of the film derives from this reflexivity, but also from the way it develops ideas about performance through acting out. The film explores thematic motifs of disaster versus success, public versus private, high culture versus low culture. The latter is elaborated in the form of tragic theatre versus popular review-style song and dance. Although there is no ingénue and no big break, the film retains the configuration of the star (Astaire) versus the producer/director (Jack Buchanan) in a conflict between both high and low culture, and film and theatre. This dynamic is further developed by Cyd Charisse, well known as a ballet dancer before entering movies. There is a clash between the two stars not only in their backgrounds but also in their performance modes – the question that fuels the narrative is: Will they be able to dance together?

Generic tropes are used. The first image we see is top hat, cane and gloves, objects which are part of the iconography of the musical but are also associated with magic acts. They are worn and become one with the body but their putting on engenders gesture and performance.

● Stern offers other examples such as the boxing gloves in *Raging Bull* (Martin Scorsese, USA, 1980) and the red shoes in *The Red Shoes* (Michael Powell and Emeric Pressburger, UK, 1948). Ask students to brainstorm other items that might be generic tropes, items which have particular meanings which connect them to a genre but which are also objects which animate or empower.

Other terms used by Lesley Stern relating to *The Band Wagon* are:

- *Histrionic and quotidian*, which describe two fundamental cinematic qualities. On the one hand, we can say that cinema since its very beginning has always had a curiosity about the quotidian, a desire to scrutinise and capture the rhythms and nuances of everyday life; on the other hand, it has been driven by a tendency to theatricalise and stylise. Histrionic cinema is at once self-conscious, ostentatious, non-naturalistic and emotionally charged and affective.
- *Daily and extra-daily*, which are used to distinguish modes of performance. The daily body is a gestural and cultural body imbued with techniques that have been absorbed and which are acted out on an unconscious and habitual level. The extra-daily body has been produced through disciplined training which enables a particular deployment of energy and includes a context, the presence of an audience and the marking out of a performance space eg, a dancer.

The Band Wagon is a film about performance that is itself performative. The film demonstrates theatre/film off-stage/on-stage links – the stage is not recreated through proscenium shots and there is no attempt to replicate the theatre audience's point of view. Theatricalisation of the cinema is achieved through other means eg, the stylised integration of décor and costumes as in Cyd Charisse's first meeting with Astaire, in which she is wearing a black dress and green gloves in a red room. This cinema says 'I love cinema and its potential to transform the world, to use colour and movement, to energise the screen so that you see new things, see differently.'

The 'Dancing in the Dark' number (one of the most celebrated Hollywood musical numbers) is the inverse of Busby Berkeley – an intimate and lyrical duet. It is magical in a highly stylised way. In terms of what we see on the screen it evokes the everyday – Fred and Cyd escape their professional lives and take a carriage into Central Park. The cinematic codes are heightened – the lighting, the sets, the painted skyline, the music and the choreography. The public/private, on-stage/off-stage tropes are animated here for narrative and performance purposes. The magical nature of the scene is explained because of the enactment of the difference between the quotidian (everyday) and the histrionic (stylised), and is also demonstrated through a transition from the daily to the 'extra-daily', in other words, normal everyday bodily activities to the bodily activities of the trained dance. It is the tension between walking and dancing – they walk through dancing couples but begin to walk in time – the walk turns into a dance.

All About Eve: Revisiting the diva gesture

All About Eve is a story set backstage in which there is no stage. Everything happens around, and in reference to, the stage: in the star's apartment, in dressing rooms, in the wings. The fact that we never see the great star, Margo Channing (Bette Davis), on stage foregrounds her performance and her star persona as cinematic, and our place as the cinema audience.

We are introduced to Margo Channing in her dressing room, the zone between the stage and the off stage. She is drinking and smoking, ordinary quotidian (everyday) activities but she performs these activities so that their gestural quality is framed – the cinema has the capacity to frame this quality. When we think of Bette Davis we think of smoking – she takes an ordinary activity and makes it fascinating. Our pleasure in watching her is partly derived from watching her recapitulation of, and variation on, performance traits she has already thoroughly demonstrated. Her performance is about performance – her gestures evoke the cinema of the divas, 'this cinema so marvellously, so properly close to theatre. There in all its glory, an arrogant female exhibitionism.'

'Fasten your seatbelts. We're in for a bumpy ride', is not simply a tired bid by a fading star but an instance of arrogant female exhibitionism in which Davis, as performer, precipitates an elaboration of the relations between 'divadom', aging, self-possession and sexuality.

Opening Night

In *Opening Night*, Gena Rowlands plays an actress (Myrtle) who is having a hard time playing on stage a woman who is having a struggle coming to terms with aging. She is confronted with a conundrum: if she identifies with the role she has been assigned and if she plays the part well, then she will be identified by her audience as old and her career will be limited. If she plays the part badly, her career and identity are also likely to be ruined. After the performance that opens the film, Myrtle is mobbed at the stage door and her attention is caught by a young adoring fan, who says 'I love you' over and over again. The fan is hit by a car and killed and reappears later as a ghost in Myrtle's breakdown.

In a more recent film, *All About My Mother* (*Todo sobre mi madre*, Pedro Almodóvar, Spain/France, 1999), Bette Davis returns, not so much as a ghost but as an iconic image (a huge poster of her blowing out smoke is in the dressing room of the theatre) and a source of inspiration. It is a film about performance, both in the more orthodox sense of stage acting and in terms of sexual identity as a process of performance. The death of the son seeking an autograph echoes the beginning of *Opening Night*. The true diva figure in *All About My Mother* tells us 'I started smoking because of Bette Davis.'

● These films all deal with performance and different aspects of identity. It may be useful to investigate such aspects as women coming to terms with aging or sexual identity and ask how they are represented on screen and through performance.

Worksheet 17: Divas and performance asks students to look at films about performance and consider how the two worlds of everyday life and performance are presented cinematically. They are also asked to look at the 'daily and extra-daily' body.

1 of 2 pages

To access student worksheets and other online materials go to *Teaching Stars and Performance* at **www.bfi.org.uk/tfms** and enter User name: **stars@bfi.org.uk** and Password: **te1302sp**.

● The Method and the Actors Studio

The performance style known as Method acting took shape in the 1930s in the work of New York's Group Theatre, where Lee Strasberg taught his version of the theories of Russian director Konstantin Stanislavski. Although others disputed Strasberg's interpretation, the 'Stanislavski system' emerged as a dominant force on the American stage after World War II, when it was principally associated with a group of performers attached to the Actors Studio in New York. Although many of its practitioners were hostile to what they saw as Hollywood's crass commercialism, an increasing number of Method-trained actors, such as Montgomery Clift, Lee J Cobb and Karl Malden, began working in the movies in the 1950s. In 1955, *On the Waterfront* (Elia Kazan, USA, 1954) won seven Academy Awards, including one for Marlon Brando for Best Actor, and the Method came to represent a demonstration of how a serious American acting performance was constructed. By the 1960s the Method had been absorbed into mainstream acting practice.

The Actors Studio, founded in New York City in 1947 by the director, Elia Kazan, Robert Lewis and Cheryl Crawford, was a workshop for professionals who wanted to develop and enhance their skills. Kazan wrote:

We decided there'd be no tuition charge and agreed to work without compensation ourselves. The only qualification for membership would be talent. No one would ever buy his way in. Our goals were modest, our principles clean.

Kazan's first love was the theatre and his dream was to revolutionise the American stage. He claimed:

The whole idea of the Group Theatre was to get poetry out of the common things in life. That was fired by the Depression and our reaction to it. Then there was another element – the Stanislavski system made us see more in the lives of human beings, and it became our mission to reveal greater depths. Also, at this time the ideas of Freud had become popularised.

The ideas that Kazan carried over from his work in theatre led him to make films that were different from the conventional films of the 1950s. More than any other director, Kazan carried the Method aesthetic into his films. This revolutionary approach to screen acting, particularly emblematised by Brando, has been the most profound influence on modern actors since the war. In 1949, Lee Strasberg became artistic director and under his command the Studio became an American temple devoted to 'the Method'.

In the 1940s and 1950s, the work of Stanislavski and his American interpreters was held up as offering a theoretical base for the profession of acting. The Method proposed 'a codifiable discipline, a teachable tradition, for acting.' It emphasised improvisation, ensemble playing, and emotional expressiveness, and it identified 'the actor's own personality not merely as a model for the creation of character but as the mine from which all psychological truth must be dug.' (*Hollywood Cinema*, Richard Maltby, 1995)

Method acting is in one sense highly visible: we are usually intensely aware of the effort involved in a Method performance. On the other hand, the Method seeks to abolish the distinction between the actor and the role, and the artificialities and histrionics of other acting techniques it sees as insincere. Method acting is not so much a technique as an approach to the creation of a performance, an approach marked by its obsession with the 'self' of the actor.

Strasberg commented that 'the actor need not imitate a human being. The actor is himself a human being and can create out of himself.' By understanding his or her own deepest anxieties and drives, the actor could produce the appropriate surface behaviour to convince the audience of the character's existence as a psychologically complex individual. In his sessions in the Actors Studio, Strasberg encouraged actors to relive or imagine an experience for themselves alone, and many of the descriptions of the Method place the acting teacher in the role of psychoanalyist.

Strasberg's method was to read out the title of a scene and the actors who were to play it. When the scene was finished he asked: 'What were you trying to do?' Then he asked the other actors what they thought. Then he delivered his own comments which were all noted by the devoted gathering.

Up to that point in time, American films had had stars like James Cagney and Spencer Tracy whose style of acting had been linked to theatrical performance. In comparison to this classical Hollywood style, the Method was relatively representational. While the classical performance sought to fulfil the requirements of the plot, the Method incorporated into its understanding of realism a sense of character as more complex and less subservient to the plot function.

The methods for character construction and impersonation advocated by Stanislavski encouraged the actor to work from within his or her own conflicts and personal experience. The star psychologically and physically becomes the role. Method actors were critical of actors such as Sir Laurence Olivier as pretenders who assume the outward appearance of parts but don't 'feel' the roles. (Olivier was irritated by Dustin Hoffman,with whom he worked on *Marathon Man* (John Schlesinger, USA, 1976), and suggested that he try acting rather than get into a 'state'.) The Method reshaped Hollywood performance and introduced the phenomenon of the star as actor which has extended into contemporary cinema.

In the 1950s actors who came to the Studio included James Dean, Marilyn Monroe, Ben Gazzara, Paul Newman and Shelley Winters. One of the studio's major discoveries was Marlon Brando. Kazan spotted him in a workshop and cast him as the lead in *A Streetcar Named Desire* on the stage and then in the film (USA, 1951). The Method subsequently came to stand for the intensive work Brando was reputed to contribute to each part such as living in a wheelchair for several weeks before playing a paraplegic in *The Men* (Fred Zinnemann, USA, 1950). His distinctive, mumbling vocal style (like a real person) was also seen as key to Method acting.

Pauline Kael described James Dean as 'the world's first teenager'. In his two 'signature' roles he is deeply personal, seeming to put his own life on view, revealing his wounds for all to see. The intimacy of his style has sustained his appeal from decade to decade. His death in 1955 has cast him forever in the role of the brooding 1950s' rebel crying out against the bland conformity-ridden world he has unwillingly inherited from his elders. He is trapped hovering on the verge of juvenile delinquency and bathed in the pain and confusion which spoke for his generation.

However, Billy Wilder criticised the Method, because when he directed *Some Like It Hot*, starring Marilyn Monroe, he got impatient with her need to 'feel' a scene which resulted in multiple takes.

The Method approach is exemplified by:

- Al Pacino in *The Godfather* (Francis Ford Coppola, USA, 1972) who uses a kind of malevolent quietness to show Michael's increasing preoccupation with his own moral decay. Mystery and ambiguity are the Method actors' stock-in-trade and they are often surrounded by an aura of meditation.
- Brando's anti-hero motorcycle gang leader in *The Wild One* (Lásló Benedek, USA, 1953).
- Brando in *Last Tango in Paris* (Bernardo Bertolucci, Italy/France, 1972) where he strips away the last layers of artifice to create the kind of expressive realism that is intensely personal and yet transcends the personal to reveal the universal. He internalises a role so that his own personality meshes with the character.
- Robert de Niro's misfit rebel in *Taxi Driver* (Martin Scorsese, USA, 1976). De Niro disappears into his characters so that there is no distance between him and the part that he is playing; the identification is so complete that the distinction between actor and role become blurred.

Worksheet 18: Comparing performances asks students to investigate traditional acting styles and those of the Method and to provide comments on performance and film language.

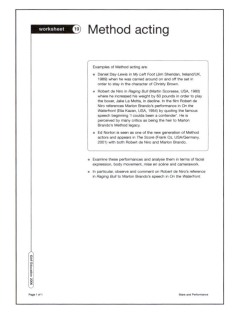

To access student worksheets and other online materials go to *Teaching Stars and Performance* at **www.bfi.org.uk/tfms** and enter User name: **stars@bfi.org.uk** and Password: **te1302sp**.

Worksheet 19: Method acting provides examples of Method acting and invites students to comment on performances in terms of facial expression and body language and to look at how the performance is supported by film language.

Strasberg remained head of the Studio until his death in 1982 and since then Al Pacino, Ellen Burstyn and others have carried it on. In the late 1990s the Actors Studio forged links with New York University offering formal drama classes for the first time. The Studio is currently famous for a televised recording of a graduate seminar called *Inside the Actors Studio* where actors and directors are interviewed. Its success has made the Actors Studio America's most popular drama school.

3

Case studies

Case study 1: Stardom and celebrity – Jennifer Aniston

Jennifer Aniston was born in Sherman Oaks, California in 1969 (her original family name was Anastassakis). Daughter to John and Nancy Aniston (both actors), she is also the god-daughter of Telly Savalas and was exposed to acting at an early age. Her family lived in Greece for a while and then returned to New York where her father played the role of the villainous Victor Kiriaki on the NBC soap opera, *Days of Our Lives*.

She attended the Rudolf Steiner School and then went on to attend New York City's High School of Performing Arts, where she was educated in Theatre and Fine Arts. She graduated in 1987 and appeared in a number of television commercials and off-Broadway productions. During this time she supplemented her income by waitressing. She moved to Los Angeles to find more lucrative work and had a number of supporting roles in failed television sitcoms eg, *Ferris Bueller* (1990), *Herman's Head* (1991), *The Edge* (1992) and *Muddling Through* (1994). She also got her first acting role in a feature film, a poorly received horror, called *The Leprechaun* (Mark Jones, USA, 1993). She then auditioned for a pilot for a series called *Friends* as the suburban princess turned waitress Rachel Green. It was a critical and commercial success and she and her co-stars became household names.

The show's success generated a wealth of media attention. She was listed in *People* magazine's 'most intriguing people' of 1995 and 1996. Her hairstyle became such a trend with American women that *Rolling Stone* named her 'America's first hairdo'.

● *Friends*

Friends ended its ten-year successful run in May 2004, but still remains one of the most popular sitcoms on television. In 2000, after a widely publicised battle with NBC, Aniston and her fellow cast members negotiated a salary of $750,000 per episode. Her celebrity status and high profile have endured, aided by her marriage to and subsequent break-up with Brad Pitt.

The series was first shown in Britain on Channel 4 in April 1995. Channel 4 had also broadcast *The Cosby Show*, *Roseanne* and *Cheers* but *Friends* was a different kind of sitcom. It wasn't set in the world of work or suburbia; it was hip, metropolitan and the scripts were littered with popular cultural references with which its target audience could identify. The characters in *Friends* were in their early twenties, American, self-obsessed, with anxieties easily recognised by their target audience. They represented a generation which was marrying less and later than any in history; they had money but no job security, lived in the city and found it hard to meet a soulmate.

Friends was funny and struck a chord with its audience. It was normal and recognisable to be directionless in love and work even in your late twenties. It also made the idea of being unattached desirable and not sad. It was an aspirational sitcom. We wanted a life like theirs – the cool New York flat with table football and easy chairs and the social circle of beautiful and supportive friends. Coffee culture also started around this time and the first New York Starbucks opened in the same year that *Friends* started (1994). The dual rise of coffee culture and *Friends* was one example of how the show captured the *Zeitgeist*. At other times it defined it. The 'Rachel' was the most copied hairstyle (since Farrah Fawcett's flick-ups).

The series has also been credited with influencing the way we speak. Researchers at Toronto University analysed the first eight episodes to explore whether popular culture had an effect on how we speak. After tabulating 9,000 adjectives, they concluded that the evidence of its effect on language could be summed up in one word: 'so'. Previously the most common way to intensify an adjective was to use 'very' or 'really'. In *Friends*, the common intensifier was 'so' and this style of speech is now more common.

More than a million *Friends* DVD boxed sets have been sold in Britain alone. Jennifer Aniston, Courteney Cox, Lisa Kudrow and Matthew Perry are all making movies, David Schwimmer is directing and Matt Le Blanc is already starring in the eponymous spin-off, *Joey* (NBC, September 2004), where he reprises his role in *Friends* in a move to Hollywood.

Most of the above information on *Friends* came from 'Inflential Friends', by Sarfaz Manzoor, The Guardian, 04/02/04.

Her appeal

In the Observer Profile (*The Observer*, 22 January 2006) Ryan Gilbey comments on Jennifer Aniston's appeal to her audiences:

> Aniston was the sparkiest member of the ensemble and the one least reliant on goofball caricature. Playing the only character with whom a sane viewer might reasonably identify also meant that she got the lion's share of attention.

He endorses this with an observation from film critic Roger Ebert:

> When I see Jennifer Aniston playing a halfway ordinary character, I have the same reaction: hey, a friend of mine has somehow gotten into the same movie with all of those stars. It's the damnedest thing.

Film career

Jennifer Aniston has tried to translate her TV stardom into success in films with romantic comedies, such as *She's the One* (1996) and *Picture Perfect* (1997) in which she had her first leading role and $2 million salary. In 1998 she played a pregnant social worker who falls for her gay friend in *The Object of My Affection* (Nicolas Hytner, USA, 1999).

Ryan Gilbey comments:

> Aniston's film career has yet to become more than an adjunct to Friends … many of Aniston's movie roles, from the career obsessive in Picture Perfect to the woman smitten with her gay best friend in The Object of My Affection have been Rachel in all but name.

When she has shown a flash of bravery, the rewards have not been plentiful. Miguel Arteta, director of *The Good Girl* (USA, 2002), in which Aniston played a dowdy shop assistant, watched the actress actively suppressing her own image

> She is a physical performer and she transformed her body for the role… She is a very happy person in real life. Her hands go up when you talk to her. And in this film she had to play someone who hated life and was kind of depressed. She wore wrist weights and ankle weight for a month before the film… (Gilbey, 2006)

The film was not particularly well received.

In her latest film *Derailed* (Mikael Håfström, USA, 2005) she plays a *femme fatale* who is raped and has an affair with a married man. It was a brave step in a new direction but one that the San Francisco Chronicle called 'a calamitous casting error'.

> There is an art to sitcom acting and she nailed it from the off. She was intimate, cheerfully conspiratorial, self-deprecating. And approachable:

whether as friend or love object, she felt within reach. … But now Aniston looks awfully lonely on that big screen, where scale is everything and the distance between performer and audience is harder to bridge. Just as Angelina Jolie, Scarlett Johansson or Charlize Theron might look ungainly squeezed into an episode of Friends so Aniston hasn't learned how to dominate the cinema screen. (Gilbey, 2006)

- It would be interesting to discuss with students whether they think that there are some stars who have an 'approachableness' or an intimacy which belongs to the medium of television and others who perform better on the cinema screen. What do they think about Gilbey's comments about Angelina Jolie and Charlize Theron?
- Take the opening sequences of a *Friends* episode and the opening sequences of *The Good Girl.* Ask students to note locations, *mise en scène*, body language. What are the differences in the roles and does Jennifer Aniston bring any qualities to the film role from her character as Rachel?

The star and her personal life

'Will Aniston merely be remembered as the woman Brad threw over for Angelina?' (*The Guardian Guide*, Preview Film, 28 January 2006)

Jennifer Aniston has been in the spotlight because of her marriage to Brad Pitt and the subsequent breakdown of the marriage, which has led to an enormous amount of publicity in magazines, on websites and talk shows, such as *Oprah Winfrey*. In September 2005 she appeared on the 20th Anniversary Oprah Winfrey show and discussed her marital break-up and her future. She expressed her desire to move on by saying to the media 'Come on people, turn a page'. The website www.people.aol.com is one example of the large number of sources of information about her private life and her new relationships.

Ryan Gilbey (ibid) quotes US website salon: 'We do not have the capacity for boredom when it comes to Jennifer Aniston and her tale of betrayal, loneliness and redemption…'

Jennifer Aniston's career, the overlapping of the roles she plays in film with the character of Rachel, together with her own persona and the public's obsession with her private life, provide interesting approaches to the concepts of the 'star as professional' and the 'star as celebrity', as examined by Christine Gledhill and Linda Williams in *Reinventing Film Studies* (2000):

- *The 'star as celebrity'* emphasises the leisure and private life of the star. Intertextuality is important since knowledge of the star's 'real' life is pieced together from gossip columns and celebrity interviews. For young fans this kind of celebrity may be the most accessible way into examining the life of a star precisely because it links together different entertainment formats – magazines, videos, photography, film. The audience has access to intimate information from a variety of sources and texts.

- *The 'star as professional'* emphasises the combination of a particular star image with a particular film context. It often involves the star's identification with a particular genre. Certain stars such as Steve Martin, Eddie Murphy and Jim Carrey are linked to comedy while Stallone, Schwarzenegger and Van Damme are associated with masculine prowess. Attention is drawn to the work of the acting so that performance and work are emphasised, not leisure and the private sphere. Film stars no longer dominate the area of celebrity status and a shift towards performance as a mark of stardom has become a way of re-establishing film star status.

- Students could research fan websites, including Jen Fans and Absolutely Jennifer Aniston or visit http://imdb.com for Jennifer Aniston's lengthy filmography as an actress, as a producer and where she has appeared as herself in programmes such as chatshows.

- Discuss how her different roles as actress, producer and being herself (in chatshows, interviews, and websites) overlap and converge. Is there a complete picture?

Worksheet 20: Star as celebrity and as professional contrasts the ideas of the celebrity and the professional and asks students to carry out some research on the 'construction' of Jennifer Aniston.

This case study helps students to examine:

- Film language
- Considerations of celebrity and stardom
- Intertextuality
- Star persona.

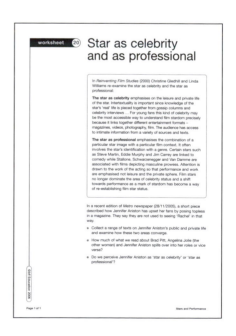

To access student worksheets and other online materials go to *Teaching Stars and Performance* at **www.bfi.org.uk/tfms** and enter User name: **stars@bfi.org.uk** and Password: **te1302sp**.

Case study 2: A particular tradition of Britishness – Hugh Grant

In *British National Cinema* (1997), Sara Street quotes Julian Petley (1985) who thought most British stars of the 1970s and 80s were too stage-bound in technique and vision. He comments on the success of Jeremy Irons and suggests that his appeal is a mixture of nostalgia for an imperial past, an obsession with failure and humiliation and a fascination with the mores (particularly sexual) of the upper classes. This description places Jeremy Irons in the established tradition of British actors, including David Niven, Michael Wilding, Kenneth More, James Fox and other such upper-class English types and anticipates the aristocratic-seeming Hugh Grant with his very similar star persona in *Four Weddings and a Funeral* (Mike Newell, UK, 1994). This particular representation has won consistent favour in America.

> Hugh Grant is an interesting example of an upper-class star whose career has been curiously assisted by his arrest in Los Angeles in 1995 with a prostitute. His persona is that of the well-bred Englishman whose off-screen behaviour merely confirms stereotypes about upper-class hypocrisy over sexual matters. Although international success has made him a star, he nevertheless comes across in interviews as a modest, stuttering, even bashful man. In turn, this behaviour has encouraged his fans to interpret 'the Divine incident' as an endearing schoolboy misdemeanour. (Sara Street, 1997)

The following information is taken from notes on *bfi* Screenonline (www.screenonline.org.uk):

● Career progression

Hugh Grant was born in 1960 and went to New College, Oxford where he began acting on stage and in films – a production of *Hamlet* in *Star Trek* uniforms and in *Privileged* (UK, 1982), a student whodunnit film directed and co-written by Michael Hoffman, who directed him much later in 1995 in *Restoration* (USA/UK). After university he appeared in some television films and in 1987 co-starred in Merchant-Ivory's' *Maurice* (UK, 1987) which led to a succession of parts such as Lord Darlington's nephew in *The Remains of the Day* (James Ivory, UK, 1993).

International success

In 1992 he played a nervous newlywed in Roman Polanski's *Bitter Moon* (France/UK), a character which he was to build on comedically in later roles and a part which helped him to get the role in *Four Weddings and a Funeral*. This changed everything for him. He has since been compared to Cary Grant in his timing and technique. This film established Grant's 'signature tics' as the mumbling, floppy-haired 'toff' and catapulted him into international success. In 2003 he received the BAFTA/LA Stanley Kubrick Britannia Award for Excellence in Film. He won a BAFTA and a Golden Globe and *Four Weddings* went on to become the highest ever grossing British film.

In 1995 he starred in *The Englishman Who Went Up a Hill but Came Down a Mountain* (Christopher Monger, USA/UK), which he followed with *Sense and Sensibility* (Ang Lee, USA). He also made an American comedy *Nine Months* (Chris Columbus, USA, 1995) and another film directed by Mike Newell in 1995 in which he played a theatre company boss, *An Awfully Big Adventure* (Ireland/UK/France/USA). In 1999 he made *Notting Hill* (Roger Michell, UK/USA, 1999), a charming feel-good romance with Julia Roberts, a major American star.

Grant's way of handling the dialogue (Richard Curtis wrote the screenplays for his two major hits), combined with his good looks, made him internationally popular. He starred in two New York comedies *Mickey Blue Eyes* (Kelly Makin, USA/UK, 1999) and *Small Time Crooks* (Woody Allen, USA, 2000). He has also played the sleazy Daniel Cleaver in the two *Bridget Jones's Diary* films (Sharon Maguire, USA/France/UK, 2001 and 2004).

Production

Simian Films, the production company that he co-owns with Elizabeth Hurley, his previous partner, was formed in October 1994 and has survived their personal separation, has allowed Grant considerable control over his choice of parts and enabled him to market himself as a particular and highly desirable commodity that can guarantee an audience. Simian Films is underwritten by Ted Turner's Castle Rock Entertainment, which provides development funds and the major finance for approved projects. Simian attempted to break into the American market with *Nine Months* and *Extreme Measures* (Michael Apted, USA/UK, 1996).

● Genre and the Hugh Grant blueprint

The next section raises issues about Hugh Grant's performances, seen by many as variations on a particular theme or stereotype, and also about the success of a particular kind of British film in relation to Hollywood and the British film industry itself. It is based on 'The Reluctance to Commit: Hugh Grant and the New British Romantic Comedy' by Andrew Spicer from *The Trouble with Men* (2004) by Phil Powrie, et al.

Cultural characteristics and popular genres

Hugh Grant is arguably the most successful current British star, famous throughout the world, able to sell a film on the strength of his name alone and commanding a $6 million fee per picture. His popularity is intertwined with a revival of British romantic comedy – a genre that has always relied on the charismatic presence of its leading actors, stars who can play comedy but who are not comedians. Like all popular genres romantic comedy uses recognisable cultural types and Grant's performances are: the flustered twit in *Four Weddings and a Funeral*, the boy next door in *Notting Hill*, the Byronic cad in *Bridget Jones's Diary* and the man about town in *About a Boy* (Chris and Paul Weitz, USA/France/UK, 2002). Andrew Spicer thinks that all these characters share a central characteristic: the reluctance, and yet the need to find one's life meaningful and central to well-being and happiness. His popularity is bound up with the comedic exploration of this dilemma although critics often deride him as a product of a debased popular taste.

Romantic comedy

Romantic comedy makes marriage the culmination of the narrative but by doing so dilutes the basic contradiction between love as an intense, all-consuming, short-lived passion and its social function as the cornerstone of stable, life-long monogamy. With its optimistic and tolerant view of life, romantic comedy has close affinities with the fairytale, which allows a magical resolution of conflicts or dilemmas, confusions and misunderstandings and provides a 'generous space' for reconciliations and forgiveness. The romance is also a process of self-discovery through which both parties come to understand their own identities.

Spicer quotes Steve Neale (1992) as noting that romantic comedy's periods of greatest success have coincided with crises in the institutions of marriage – in a post-Aids, post-feminist era of accelerating divorce rates, where there is a general scepticism about marriage and commitment, romantic comedy provides a legitimate space for the confident embrace of an idealised romantic union. Following an American revival in the late 1980s and 1990s, romantic comedy is now more popular than ever.

According to Spicer, Frank Krutnik (1998) claims that contemporary romantic comedy's idealisation of love has a characteristically postmodern playfulness, a knowing mockery of genre conventions. He contends that 'in an age of lost innocence' writers and filmmakers are able to speak the language of love through foregrounding generic conventions as conventions which allow their message to be articulated in the context of a self-protective irony. Audiences are invited to recognise the fabrication, but also to emotionally endorse the sentiment: 'to love the lie'.

Contemporary masculinity

Andrew Spicer suggests that Hugh Grant's films and persona are layered with such self-protective irony, but also that his performances are geared to reveal the ambiguities and insecurities of contemporary masculinity. Insecurity and lack of confidence (with the partial exception of *Bridget Jones*) are the defining characteristics of Grant's characters, who are social and career failures, reluctant to commit themselves to the potentially powerful hazards of romantic union. This insecurity is generic – his role is to explore a particular type of English inhibition and reserve, 'how embarrassing and funny it is to be English' (Hugh Grant quoted in Chadhuri, 1994/Spicer, 2004).

> Hugh Grant's star image, which has changed and developed more than is generally recognised, has made ... an important contribution to the construction of contemporary masculinity, reanimating popular archetypes in a renewed bid for the cultural hegemony of the middle class. (Spicer, 2004)

Although he is a popular icon of middle-class Englishness, Hugh Grant's success has also been criticised, partly through his association with romantic comedy, which is usually perceived as a conservative genre reaffirming monogamous, heterosexual love as the social norm and family life as the ultimate fulfilment. Also, *Four Weddings* and *Notting Hill* have been attacked as nostalgic and disingenuous, avoiding the realities of contemporary Britain in favour of a fey, middle-class never-never land. Grant's persona has been criticised as insular and reactionary.

In the *Independent on Sunday* Profile (14 November 2004), Neil Norman comments that

> Hugh Grant has become the only young British male movie star worthy of international recognition. He cracked Hollywood and endeared himself to international audiences with a particular persona that is more David Niven than Cary Grant: he possesses a charm that is actually heightened on the screen ...

He goes on to explain the subtlety of Hugh Grant's 'blueprint':

> To cite the Hugh Grant blueprint – that he always plays the same stereotype – as an example of his limitations as an actor is folly. This is a persona that has been thrust upon him. Once audiences have identified a movie star with a particular screen persona it is brutally difficult to persuade them of alternative aspects. In fact, close study reveals a wealth of tiny nuances within each one that shade and alter the basic formula for each film.

Cultural types: Self-deprecatingly English

In *Four Weddings*, Hugh Grant draws upon a familiar cultural type – the well-bred but hopelessly repressed, tongue-tied, awkward and self-deprecating Englishman. His floppy-haired gaucheness and his stammering, together with the ability to be surprised by almost everything, remind us of P G Wodehouse's Bertie Wooster. However, the good looks and charm are those of a leading man. Hugh Grant's performance was summed up as a

> small marvel of acute observation, a credible amalgamation of flustered faux pas, timid lust, embarrassed ineptitude and confused emotional awakenings. (Andrews, 1994, quoted by Spicer, 2004)

Richard Curtis, who wrote the original screenplay, thought Grant's greatest strength, aside from his good looks, was the ability to speak his lines with an 'exuberant naturalism' that made a plausible and three-dimensional character from the exaggeration and caricature that is often the staple of comedy.

Four Weddings was modestly budgeted and hugely successful earning £27.7 million and becoming at this point the highest-grossing British film ever. Competent marketing in the USA allowed it to build an audience. British audiences seemed to enjoy Grant's flustered foppishness and American women saw him as the quintessence of diffidence and old-world charm. Unlike the stars of American comedy, Grant was fey without being gay, his sexuality built upon wit and irony. Sheila Johnston judged his success the triumph of 'wimp power', a backlash against the stone-face action hero which had been the dominant male type.

> Four Weddings made him a truly international star whose image was promoted in tabloid newspaper articles, television chatshows and magazine profiles. (Johnston, 1994, quoted by Spicer, 2004)

His interviews confirmed his romantic attractiveness, his good looks, his floppy hair and charming smile and his impeccable manners. He also exuded glamour, especially through his high-profile relationship with model and actress Elizabeth Hurley. They were a celebrity couple in the 1990s.

- Students might like to explore some of the Hugh Grant websites and look at what they contain, what differentiates them and what comments/exchanges take place.
- Are they different in what they want to present about the star? They could also collect examples of tabloid and broadsheet reviews/reports, magazine articles, and television interviews and appearances in order to analyse both the attitudes of different aspects of the media to the star and, at the same time, how all these different, fragmented views also construct the persona of the star.
- If students have done work on Britishness and masculinity (see page 41), they could consider Hugh Grant's place as a 'British hero'. Does he represent men in British society today? What other examples of British men in film can they find?

Everyman – an ordinary bloke: Notting Hill

Notting Hill was released in May 1999. Working Title, an independent company backed by the financial resources, distributional and promotional power of a major studio (Polygram), marketed and exhibited the film like an American blockbuster (the same strategy was used for *Bridget Jones* and *About a Boy*). *Notting Hill* was even more successful than *Four Weddings* grossing £30.7 million in the UK and $116 million in the USA.

Whereas *Four Weddings* caricatured the debonair gentleman in Home Counties' England, Grant's William Thacker is 'an ordinary bloke', a humdrum middle-class divorcé who leads a 'strange half-life' as he puts it in the opening voiceover – a narrative device that creates a strong identification between character and audience – wittily self-deprecating about his problems. William is offered as an Everyman, the quintessentially decent boy next door. His everyday normality is underscored by the comic excess of his flatmate, played by slovenly Rhys Ifans, and the gauche shop assistant. In a gender reversal, Anna is the competitive high achiever while the under-achieving William plays the woman's traditional role as the one who waits and suffers.

Notting Hill is also more confident in its handling of genre conventions. Curtis has observed that 'The film is a concealed fairytale – the Princess and the Woodcutter'. The Princess is a Hollywood movie star, with Julia Roberts, the most successful American female star of the 1990s, playing 'herself' as Anna Scott.

Britain and America are contrasted particularly through the boorishness of Anna's boyfriend Jeff with William's gentle diffidence and also by Anna's return to the bookshop stating that the fame thing (the Hollywood star persona) 'isn't really real' and presenting herself as 'just a girl standing in front of a boy, asking him to love her.' William hesitates and expresses his feelings in the most public of spheres, which counters the sentimental ending of the pregnant couple in an idyllic garden setting.

Hugh Grant's 'New Man' presents a tolerant and caring alternative to the macho tough guy. The New Man's sensitivity, desiring a committed relationship with the opposite sex over career ambition, allows him to embrace positively feminine roles and qualities, and embody values central to the critique of traditional competitive masculinity. Traditional male roles have been patriarchal and competitive, eg, competing in the workplace as the breadwinner, the father who provides for the family, the winning sportsman. The insecurities and confusions about manliness felt by contemporary middle-class Englishmen are contained in this liberal response to the rising aspirations and assertiveness of women. If you are nice, fundamentally decent and easy-going, that will win the day.

Sexual predator

In pre-publicity for *Bridget Jones's Diary*, Grant was fanfared in the tabloids as 'No More Mr Nice Guy' and photographed in women's magazines bare-chested in tight leather trousers to reveal his new leaner and more muscular body. In *Bridget Jones*, he plays the predatory boss at the publishing house, contrasting with Mark Darcy playing the repressed Englishman, an uptight human rights lawyer. Colin Firth (Mark Darcy) had been very popular in his portrayal of Mr Darcy in the successful BBC television adaptation of *Pride and Prejudice* and audiences would recognise this counter-casting.

Bridget Jones was another huge hit grossing over £42 million at the UK box office (Dyja, 2002). Grant's performance was praised:

> Playing a creep with no morals he excels. As Bridget's caddishly concupiscent boss and later boyfriend, Grant's Wodehousian twittishness is enhanced with a womanising leer and curdled suavity. No woman could resist him *(Andrews, 2001)*.

His charismatic presence complicates the straightforward romantic plot and ensures that he will be in the sequel.

New man and new lad

About a Boy is an adaptation of Nick Hornby's 1998 bestseller. Hornby's distinction has been to create a particular version of the modern male who occupies that fraught and uncertain space between the two dominant constructions of contemporary masculinity: New Man and New Lad. His middle-class anti-heroes have an awareness of feminism and a self-reflexivity about their masculinity, are sensitive, in touch with their emotions and introspective, almost neurotic. But they also cling to old modes of masculine behaviour, exhibiting laddish traits of self-centredness, the obsessive pursuit of 'hobbies' and an often chauvinistic view of women.

Grant's image was transformed for his role as Will Freeman. His hair short and spiky, he sports a range of designer T-shirts and jackets. His accent less upper class than usual with flatter vowels as he comments with acerbic wit on his own situation. He is the man-about-town archetype – sophisticated, witty, urbane, at leisure. He is proud that having reached his late 30s he has formed no long-term commitments. His role as adviser to a young boy develops and he undergoes a moral awakening from selfishness to caring responsibility. In the process he becomes aware of his own emptiness and his fears and self-doubts are far deeper than those of former Grant characters. He seems to have 'an existential terror at his own lack of identity' – 'I'm blank. I'm nothing'. His redemption comes through emotional commitment to Marcus, which prepares the ground for a new, settled relationship in an affirmation of love, commitment, responsibility, parenthood and caring for others.

Reviewers praised Grant's performance saying that he had made an essentially shallow character interesting and appealing. Impeccable timing, precise delivery, expression – all combined to create a complex portrait of self-centredness, acerbic wit, coupled with blankness and doubt. This is an image that he played to in interview expressing his own fears of becoming the 'oldest swinger in town'. *About a Boy* did well in the UK with a gross of £16.5 million but for American audiences it lacked the presence of a Hollywood star and the romantically upbeat ending.

● Britishness and Hollywood hegemony

Andrew Spicer comments that much of the criticism of Hugh Grant and the genre of films he appears in reflects a political correctness that is embarrassed by popular sentiment and optimistic fantasy, especially as they seem to be complicit with Hollywood's cultural hegemony. Academic criticism of British cinema has generally been much more comfortable with films about the alienated and the oppressed, with sombre social realism or with subversive genres (horror and crime) that support transgressing images of masculinity. However, the author quotes Judith Williamson who acknowledges that these films provide for the public a broad framework through which strong emotions may be dealt with – 'failure and insecurity and hesitation: about the pain of emotionally screwing up'. He argues that Grant's characters' discovery of 'true love' allows audiences to feel comfortable about a difficult area of modern living – the problem of commitment. They provide a way for under-achieving and insecure males to feel good about themselves and for women to entertain dreams of a sensitive caring soul mate.

Worksheet 21: Working Title
asks students to look at a range of comments about and reviews of *Four Weddings and a Funeral* and *Notting Hill*, to consider the differing opinions and to comment on why they think these films were so successful.

This case study is useful for an examination of:
● British stars
● Representation of the Britishness over time
● Genre
● Britain and Hollywood.

To access student worksheets and other online materials go to *Teaching Stars and Performance* at **www.bfi.org.uk/tfms** and enter User name: **stars@bfi.org.uk** and Password: **te1302sp**.

1 of 2 pages

Case study 3: Stars and representation – Will Smith

Will Smith is a popular contemporary star who works in a variety of media, as well as film, and who has successfully made himself popular with young black and white audiences. This case study begins with a brief overview of the history of black people in Hollywood, based on Wendy Hewing's paper for a workshop session at National Film Theatre: 'Blacks in Hollywood', October 2004.

- In Hollywood in the early 1900s black actors in leading roles or any roles were practically non-existent. Black roles of the silent film era consisted almost entirely of white actors and actresses portraying black people 'blacking up' with make-up. In the early 1920s and 1930s many black actors and actresses played roles of the servant, 'mammie', coon and the mocked and often clumsy fool. Actors like Steppin' Fetchit and Hattie McDaniel were two actors at the time who paved the way for others, though they were often criticised – many local and national organisations often believed that black movie actors should not perpetuate the negative attitude white people had towards black people. Hollywood's decision-makers often overlooked social and economic considerations and much that was circulated about race behaviour was propaganda. Black actors and actresses were either accused of not having dramatic capabilities or of not having stories to interest audiences or to make money for the filmmakers. This left the struggling group to minimal, degrading roles.

- In the 1920s and 30s a small group of black artists began to diversify and emerge overseas. They began producing films, as well as acting and others performed in nightclubs. Among these entertainers were Paul Robeson, Lena Horne and Louis Armstrong. A well-known black composer Phil Moore worked with several studios and Oscar Micheaux Jr emerged as one of the greatest producers of African-American films. He developed and produced projects outside Hollywood and helped fuel the hopes of many black actors and actresses such as Dorothy Dandridge, who was one of Hollywood's greatest female actors. Oscar Micheaux (1884–1951) was the son of former slaves. He directed and produced 35 films between 1918 and 1948. He survived in a hostile economic and racist system and dealt with themes neglected and forbidden in Hollywood films – racism, lynchings, skin colour and black success myths. He refused to present sterile and despairing blacks.

- *Gone with the Wind* (Victor Fleming, USA, 1939) produced by David Selznick. Adapted from a hugely successful novel, the film conveys nostalgia for old-world gentility and social order and the glories of the old South. It includes stereotypes of black people and Hattie McDaniel plays Mammie, who won an Oscar as Best Supporting Actress. Black organisations protested against the film which they found offensive and there were pickets and sit downs across the USA. Black actors were not allowed into the Atlanta premiere.

● The 1960s saw the growth of the Civil Rights Movement and Martin Luther King's advocacy of non-violent integrationist policies. *Guess Who's Coming to Dinner* (Stanley Kramer, USA, 1967) starred Sidney Poitier, who had been the first black man to receive an Oscar for *Lilies of the Field* (Ralph Nelson, USA) in 1963. The films showed optimistic and non-violent attitudes to racial tensions and reflected the goal of racial harmony. It has the first interracial screen kiss and was the biggest box-office hit of the year. Sidney Poitier began to play roles which were about his race. In *In the Heat of the Night* he plays an intelligent, educated, well-spoken police officer. In 1968, Martin Luther King and Malcolm X were assassinated which led to feelings of despair, riots and a hardening of attitudes on both sides. Militancy increased and the Black Panthers and Angela Davis proposed 'separatist' policies.

● The 1970s were a breakthrough for black actors – a new wave of blaxploitation films with new images for black audiences. For example, in 1971 *Shaft* (Gordon Paris, USA) appeared with its streetwise, confident and anti-hero cop who was both sexy and successful. However, the films were largely written by white Hollywood scriptwriters and did present caricatures. They were made to construct new audiences for an ailing Hollywood. The remake of *Shaft* in 2000 starring Samuel Jackson and directed by John Singleton deals overtly with race: Shaft is involved with a racially motivated murder.

● Hollywood seems to have responded to the black liberal movement in two ways: with the production of the historical anti-racist films such as *Cry Freedom* (Richard Attenborough, UK, 1987), *Malcolm X* (Spike Lee, USA, 1992) and with the development of the blaxploitation genre characters such as *Shaft* and *Black Caesar* (Larry Cohen, USA, 1973) showed black individuals as the central protagonists and in control in contrast to the marginal roles they had played previously. However, white members of society maintain a sense of intellectual and moral superiority. These films are veiled with black cool but there are still traces of the primitive stereotype; blacks tend to be the most cunning, frightening and glamorous crooks.

The apparent empowerment of black people still denotes an essence of white moral superiority.

Black actors and directors in contemporary film

- *Spike Lee* is a black American director and producer of independent films – he acts, produces and edits. *She's Gotta Have It* was made on a minimal budget in 1986. It won the Jeunesse Award at Cannes in 1986. *Do the Right Thing* (Spike Lee, 1989) was nominated for an Oscar for its screenplay. Race and racism is at the centre of his films and he also deals with the relationships between blacks and other ethnicities. In the two decades since Cannes praised his work he has never been awarded a prize in his own country or been nominated for an Oscar in the best director category (Ang Lee is the first non-white director to win one). Denzel Washington starred in Spike Lee's film *Malcolm X*, which made him a Hollywood star. He has collaborated with Spike Lee in four films and the latest is *Inside Man*, 2006, a big budget heist movie. The film comments on racism in New York (a Sikh hostage is ignorantly identified as an Arab) and the infatuation with violence and gangsta rap among the black community. Spike Lee's second film to come out in 2006 is a documentary on the hurricane *Katrina – When the Levees Broke*.

- *Denzel Washington* is one of the biggest black box-office stars. His image is thoughtful, honest, committed and decent. He won the Best Supporting Actor Academy Award for *Glory* (Edward Zwick) in 1989 and in 2002 he made film history with Halle Berry as they both won Best Actor (*Training Day*, Antoine Fuqua, 2001) and Actress (*Monster's Ball,* Marc Forster, 2001) Academy Awards. Will Smith had also been nominated for *Ali* (Michael Mann, 2001). Washington's acceptance speech paid homage to Sidney Poitier who won an honorary Oscar at the same Awards ceremony.

- Students could search the internet for and study the two acceptance speeches by Denzel Washington and Halle Berry. What are their feelings about being black actors?

- Spike Lee is also an interesting subject for case study work; he has worked both in the independent and mainstream sectors of Hollywood as director and actor. Students may like to follow themes in his work in both sectors.

● Will Smith

Willard Christopher Smith Junior was born in 1968 in West Philadelphia. His father was a former air force pilot who ran his own refrigerator business. His mother worked for the Philadelphia school board. The household was quite strict (his father had a military background) and the neighbourhood was racially mixed:

I grew up in a Baptist household, went to a Catholic school, lived in predominantly Jewish neighbourhood and hung out with Muslim kids. (quoted in The Observer, Paul Harris, 4 August 2004)

Will Smith has multiple career strands:

The rapper

- At 12 Will Smith met Jeff Townes and they began making demo tapes with the goal of emulating their heroes Run DMC. The family valued education and Will Smith was offered a place at the Massachusetts Institute of Technology which he turned down to pursue a promising musical career.

- At 20, Will Smith produced the Grammy award winning album 'He's the DJ, I'm the Rapper' with hit songs such as 'Girls Ain't Nothing but Trouble' and 'Parents Just Don't Understand' which became cult hits not just for the content but for the comic overtones. He came to stand for a new group of rappers who did not use explicit language or violence. Bands such as Public Enemy had caused controversy with profanity-laced lyrics. Smith and Townes became the acceptable face of rap. White audiences liked it, too, and Smith became a crossover star.

- In 1998 he did an interview with Barbara Walters, in which he criticised other rappers for encouraging young people to speak in 'ebonics' (a black dialect) instead of correct English.

The actor

- Smith's ambition drove him to approach Bunny Medina about pursuing an acting career. The concept of The Fresh Prince of Bel-Air (a television series about a wealthy black family in California who take in a poor relation played by Will Smith) was based on Medina's life – he was born poor and went to live with a rich Beverly Hills family. The idea was pitched to NBC who brought Quincy Jones in as a producer. The show was extremely successful and lasted for six years before Smith decided to leave it.

- His success on television led to his first big acting role in Six Degrees of Separation (Fred Schepisi, USA, 1994) which was acclaimed as an impressive performance for a first role. The subject matter was dark (Smith played a homosexual con artist) and he was aware that his film roles might have an effect on the image he projected through his music. It was a huge risk for a young black actor and Smith backed out of a gay kiss on camera for fear it would harm future roles.

- He turned to action films such as Bad Boys (Michael Bay, USA, 1995) in which he played a wise-cracking cop which was a blockbuster hit and the enormously successful Independence Day (Roland Emmerlich, USA) in 1996, which established him on the same level as Tom Hanks and Tom Cruise in terms of asking fees. He is now one of Hollywood's most bankable stars. Another hit was Men in Black (Barry Sonnerfeld, USA, 1997), for which he also provided the title song.

- He married Jada Pinkett a black actress in 1996 and also made another successful album called 'Big Willie Style'.
- His first cinematic failure was *Wild Wild West* (Barry Sonnenfeld, USA, 1999) although it was financially successful at the box office. He released another successful album in 1999, called Willennium, and received three American Music Awards.
- In *I Robot* (Alex Proyass, USA, 2004), another hit film, his love interest is a white actress. Pairing a black man and a white woman in Hollywood is still rare but it was hardly mentioned. Smith's image is rich polite, charming – 'the ultimate in crossover appeal' (The Observer, ibid). He seems to be the one man in America for whom race does not matter. Only in the title role in the boxing biopic *Ali* did Smith overtly play a black man, a historical figure. He was nominated for an Academy Award for this role.

In terms of identity in his roles it is unlikely that audiences remember the names of any of the characters he plays: he is loved for being Will Smith.

> The lines of ethnicity and skin colour are still sharply drawn across America and that is reflected in the mirror of Hollywood. Black actors often get paid less than white counterparts. Their roles are more narrowly defined. They are often black first, actors second … His success is colour-blind and for the privilege he is paid $20 million a movie. Audiences love him in equal measure, whether they are men or women, black or white … Is he a black triumph in a white world? (Observer, ibid 2004)

- Discuss with students what it is that makes Will Smith so popular and why he pleases such a wide audience.

● Racial representations

We have looked at Will Smith as star, rapper and as a black actor in Hollywood. Here we take a closer look at what it is he may represent to a number of audiences. Cultural Studies gives us a theoretical framework for racial representations. For example, Stuart Hall (*Policing the Crisis*, 1978) outlines three basic images in the 'grammar of race' employed in old movies:

- Slave: shown as dependable and devoted to his master, thus allowing the audience to displace guilt about the history of colonialism and slavery. For example, a mammy with rolling eyes or a faithful fieldhand, willing to serve his master, such as the black slaves in *Gone with the Wind* (Victor Fleming, USA, 1939).
- Native: the slave is simultaneously depicted as unpredictable and capable of turning nasty by, for example, coming out of the darkness and kidnapping the children or slaying the heroine. This primitivism justifies their servile positions and the white man's position of control. *King Kong* (Merian C Cooper, Ernest B Schoedsack, USA, 1933) is a good example.

- Clown or entertainer: 'the ignorant darkie whose life revolved around song and dance perpetuating the myth that blacks were happy with their slave status' (source as above). According to Hall, the image of Sambo is one of the most enduring and pervasive representations of black people in the history of the media. He suggests that black sitcoms have normalised black subjugation by reflecting an acknowledgement of a rising black middle class and representing black people in a non-threatening way to white audiences. However, such sitcoms perpetuate the myth of the black clown: the distinction is never made about whether we are laughing with or at the clown.

In contrast, on the website, Wikipedia, it is claimed that while the American TV series, *The Fresh Prince of Bel-Air* (NBC 1990) is largely a comedy, the show does address serious African-American issues. (The series shows how a wealthy family living in Bel-Air, California, receives a dubious gift from their poorer relations in Philadelphia when Will Smith arrives to live with them. His mother wants him to learn some good old-fashioned values from his successful relatives, but Will disrupts the sophisticated serenity of Bel-Air with his streetwise common sense.) These are some of the issues that the show addresses:

- *Black identity:* Will accuses his uncle of having forgotten 'where he came from' and discusses Malcolm X; Will and Carlton try to join an all-black fraternity, but Carlton is singled out as a sell-out because his family is wealthy and 'acts white'.
- *Gun laws:* They discuss carrying guns for self-defence.
- *Absent fathers:* Will finally meets his father in a particularly emotional episode and confronts his grief when his father abandons him for a second time.
- *Teenage pregnancy.*
- *Interracial marriages:* Will's aunt announces her engagement to a white man.
- *Drug use:* Will has trouble staying awake for basketball, finals and his girlfriend and considers drug use, but Carlton takes the amphetamines by mistake.

- You may wish to discuss with students Stuart Hall's idea of the clown or entertainer and the claims that *Fresh Prince* does address African-American issues. Which do they most agree with?

Worksheet 22: Will Smith's image and character asks students to look at the roles that Will Smith plays, to consider them in terms of black representation and to prepare a case study of one other black actor.

To access student worksheets and other online materials go to *Teaching Stars and Performance* at **www.bfi.org.uk/tfms** and enter User name: **stars@bfi.org.uk** and Password: **te1302sp**.

1 of 2 pages

White people still dominate the means of production in the television and film industries and although producers and directors may consider themselves to be liberal individuals in trying to bring race issues to the screen or for avoiding traditional stereotypes, they still largely rely on racial stereotypes they have assimilated as white people living in a racist society, for example, when investigative journalism looks at young blacks and identity they very often interview them in the context of crime or failing in school. Deliberate attempts at presenting positive black images tend to be based on normative American ideals; for example in *The Cosby Show* (NBC, 1984), there is nothing specifically 'black' about the Huxtables' lifestyle.

People, ideas and events are presented to us through media texts in a process which actively constructs meanings about the world and re-presents them. Representation is a key concept across Film and Media Studies, offering a way to study the meanings and values which films and other media texts offer. We can investigate who is being represented in terms of age, gender, class, religion, ethnicity and sexuality and how they are represented in terms of cultural and technical codes. In an investigation of both widely circulated media texts and other representations Richard Dyer (in *TV and Schooling*, eds D Lusted and P Drummond 1985) asked the following questions:

- What sense of the world is it (the media text) making?
- What does it imply is typical of the world and what deviant?
- Who is speaking? For whom? To whom?
- What does it represent to us and why? How do we respond to this representation of the world?

We can develop these questions further:

- What kind of world does the text construct?
- How could it claim to be typical of that world?
- Whose values and beliefs are being expressed through the ideas of the text?
- Who is the intended audience?
- Who will make meaning out of the text and to what purpose?
- Do these representations challenge or reaffirm our understanding of the world in the way it appears to be?

Worksheet 23: Will Smith and representation asks students to consider these questions of representation in terms of Will Smith in his various roles.

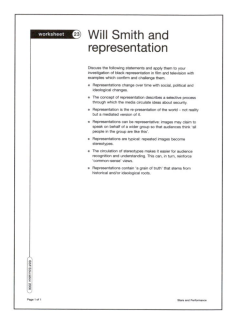

To access student worksheets and other online materials go to *Teaching Stars and Performance* at **www.bfi.org.uk/tfms** and enter User name: **stars@bfi.org.uk** and Password: **te1302sp**.

● Will Smith, the New Hollywood and synergy

This section is based on Paul McDonald, *The Star System* (2000).

Genre hybrids in Hollywood

Paul McDonald quotes Thomas Schatz (1993) in his discussion of the New Hollywood where many of the most successful films in the contemporary market have been characterised by a hybrid mixing of generic conventions. Where the classic Hollywood cinema of the studio era maintained clear generic differences, contemporary Hollywood has produced films which freely combine aspects of several genres. *Star Wars* (George Lucas, 1977), for example, combines science fiction, the Western, the war film and the adventure movie.

This breadth of generic references can be related to the marketability of the high-concept or event movie. By offering a taste of many things, something for everybody, a single film can maximise its audience. Schatz suggests that contemporary cinema displays 'purposeful incoherence', providing an intentional combination of pleasures which 'opens' the film to different readings (and readers) allowing for multiple interpretative strategies and thus broadening the potential audience.

Horizontal integration and synergy

In the entertainment business, horizontal integration has conjured up belief in the power of 'synergy'. Synergy is a buzzword of modern marketing and describes the opportunity to sell a single property or concept across several markets in ways that provide for the interaction and synchronisation of promotional energies. Mixing ownership of film rights with assets in television production and broadcasting, together with their own consumer product licensing divisions, the horizontally integrated media and entertainment conglomerates are ideally placed to see returns from numerous revenue streams relating to a single property. The promotion of a film may sell its soundtrack on an album, toys and other merchandising, and later a television spin-off. Through synergy, stars can be used to market a property across different media.

Sony Pictures Entertainment (SPE) made effective use of Will Smith around the promotion of *Men in Black*. As a hybrid mixture of comedy, action, science fiction and conspiracy theory narratives, the film entertained a broad spectrum of tastes across both child and adult audiences. The identity of Will Smith was primarily used to sell the *Men in Black* concept across various media. His fame as rap artist, comic television actor and solo singer supported this perfectly. Prior to the opening of SPE's *Men in Black* in the United States during the summer season of 1997, Sony Music Entertainment (SME) released Smith's single of the same name. With a video featuring extracts from the movie, song and film served to mutually promote each other. The image of 'Men in Black', the black-suited heroes in sunglasses, appeared across posters and other promotional materials to brand the film with a noirish but highly glossy style. This uniform style is central to the marketability of the high concept property. Will Smith's racial identity is also important – his colour and his background in rap makes 'blackness' a factor in marketing the film as 'hip'. The look of the film was intimately linked with the star.

The formula does not always work: *Wild Wild West*, a hybrid mixture of genres, with Will Smith in the lead role and supported by his soundtrack single did not match the performance of the previous phenomenon, grossing $114 million in North America, and $104 million internationally, compared with *Men in Black*'s $250 million in North America and $313 million overseas.

Will Smith's synergy is uncharacteristic of modern stardom. The crossing over of music and film careers is more representative of a previous era of stars such as Bing Crosby, Doris Day and Frank Sinatra. Disney also markets animated features across many media and consumer products.

Use **Worksheet 24: Cross marketability** to explore these issues with students.

To access student worksheets and other online materials go to *Teaching Stars and Performance* at **www.bfi.org.uk/tfms** and enter User name: **stars@bfi.org.uk** and Password: **te1302sp**.

● **Highlights from a multi-media career**

1988   DJ Jazzy Jeff and the Fresh Prince release their breakthrough LP, 'He's the DJ, I'm the Rapper', selling over three million copies in the US. They win the first MTV Music Award.

1989   DJ Jazzy Jeff and the Fresh Prince win a Grammy Award for best rap performance for 'Parents Just Don't Understand'.

1990   *The Fresh Prince of Bel-Air* sitcom for NBC.

1991   DJ Jazzy Jeff and the Fresh Prince hit the top 40 with 'Summertime' and 'Ring My Bell'.

1992   DJ Jazzy Jeff and the Fresh Prince win a second Grammy for Best Rap Performance Duo or Group for 'Summertime'.

1993   Smith appeared in *Six Degrees of Separation* and his performance was acclaimed.

       Jazzy Jeff and the Fresh Prince release their last studio LP, 'Code Red'. The song 'Boom! Shake the Room' was a hit and the LP increased their street credibility with fans.

1995   Will Smith stars in *Bad Boys*.

1996   Stars in the blockbuster: *Independence Day*.

1997   Hits the top 10 with 'Men in Black' and the film topped the box office for the summer. He won a MTV Video Music Award for Best Video from a Film (*Men in Black*)

Releases 'Big Willie Style', selling over four million copies by the autumn of 1998.

1998   Wins his first solo Grammy award for Best Rap Solo Performance.

Wins two MTV video music awards for Best Male Video ('Just the Two of Us').

Enemy of the State is a hit.

1999   Wins his fourth Grammy Award for Best Rap Performance ('Getting Jiggy with It'). Wins a MTV video music award for Best Male Video ('Miami').

2000   Wins an American music award for Favourite Male Artist.

Wins World Music Awards for world's best-selling male pop artist, male R'n'B artist and male rap artist. Stars in *The Legend of Bagger Vance* with Matt Damon.

2001   *Ali* broke Christmas Day box-office records

2002   Nominated for a Golden Globe Award and for an Academy Award for Best Actor in a Drama for *Ali*. (Denzel Washington wins.)

2004   Stars in *I, Robot* and is heard in the animated feature *Shark Tale*.

2005   Hosts and performs at the Live 8 concert in his home town, Philadelphia, on 2 July.

This case study should be useful in helping students look at:
- The history of black actors in Hollywood
- Cultural representations
- Cross marketability
- Representation in general

Case study 4: Directing actors – Mike Leigh

Information in this section is drawn from *The World According to Mike Leigh* by Michael Coveney, 1996, and *Naked and Other Screenplays*, 1995, which includes *Mike Leigh: an interview with Graham Fuller*.

Mike Leigh was born in Salford in 1943, a doctor's son of Russian Jewish descent. He attended Salford Grammar School and at 17 won a scholarship to RADA. He also studied at the Camberwell College of Art and the Central School of Art and Design before enrolling at the London Film School. In 1967 he was appointed assistant director at the RSC and in 1971 he released his first feature film *Bleak Moments*, but did not make a second film until *High Hopes* in 1988. He came to prominence in 1977 with the stage and TV drama *Abigail's Party*, which was voted one of the 100 best plays of the past millennium. He was awarded an OBE in 1990. In Cannes, he won the Palme d'Or in 1996 for *Secrets and Lies* and the director's prize in 1993 for *Naked*. At the Venice Film Festival, *Vera Drake* (2004) won the Golden Lion and Imelda Staunton won the award for best actress. The film was also nominated for Academy Awards for Original Screenplay, Actress in a Leading Role and Director.

In his interview with Graham Fuller, Mike Leigh comments on his background:

> I was born in a working-class part of North Salford, Lancashire, in 1943, into a world that was characterized by its day-to-day ordinariness, its industrial grime, before the Clean Air Act. My father was a doctor, and we lived over the surgery ... I was ... a middle-class kid growing up in a working-class environment, so I have an awareness of and sensitivity to both those worlds – I suppose I was an insider and an outsider all at once. There are certain atmospheres and images and events – and particular characters and relationships and tensions – that go right through my work, and can be traced to one or other of these aspects of my background.

● Influences and inspirations

In 1960 he left school and got a scholarship to RADA to train as an actor and moved to London. One of the first films he saw when he came to London was John Cassavetes' *Shadows* (USA, 1959) and for the first time he felt it might be possible to create complete plays from scratch with a group of actors. Leigh was fascinated by a production, in 1960, of Harold Pinter's *The Caretaker*. 'It just seemed so real.' He directed the play in his second year at RADA.

Of cinema he says:

> I saw anything and everything ... suddenly, there was Jack Clayton's Room at the Top (1958) ... the real world that one actually lived in seemed to me exciting and extraordinary in its stark, grey reality – and it was incredibly inspiring to see this same world up there on the screen for the first time.

> Among the most important things that happened to me was the discovery of world cinema. I started to look at films from all over the place – Eisenstein, Renoir, de Sica, Satyajit Ray, the Japanese cinema, the French New Wave, Buster Keaton and in the theatre, Beckett and Pinter, Brecht, Joan Littlewood and Peter Brook.

> Those things opened up all kinds of doors ... there was also the New Wave cinema ... virtually every one of them was adapted from a book or a play; the other was that there was something about them which I'm not sure I could have put my finger on at the time, that wasn't quite the living cinema that I have an instinct for ... Some people have related my films to those of Cassavetes, but I think we're very different. He was more of an inspiration than an influence.

**Worksheet 25: Mike Leigh –
Influences and inspirations** asks
students to carry out brief research
on one of the influences mentioned
and to pinpoint which aspects of
the work may have inspired Mike
Leigh.

To access student worksheets and
other online materials go to *Teaching
Stars and Performance* at
www.bfi.org.uk/tfms and enter
User name: **stars@bfi.org.uk** and
Password: **te1302sp**.

● **Style and tradition**

Mike Leigh's films carry the central themes of family secrets and mysteries
boiling to the surface. He is admired for his gritty, downbeat studies of working
lives and the wretched absurdities of class. This came first in television plays –
notably in *Abigail's Party*, set in the suburbs in the 1970s and then in the late
1980s and 90s in feature films, devised, like all his work, through improvisation
and typified by what his fans see as vivid neo-Dickensian life, which his
detractors dismiss as caricature and 'miserabilism'.

> My ongoing preoccupation is with families, relationships, parents,
> children, sex, work, surviving, being born and dying. I'm totally intuitive,
> emotional, subjective, empirical, instinctive. I'm not an intellectual film-
> maker. Primarily, my films are a response to the way people are, to the
> way things are as I experience them. In a way they are acts of taking the
> temperature. (Mike Leigh, International Herald Tribune, 2 March 1994)

He also says

> I know I return endlessly to preoccupations, but you're not necessarily
> aware that you do. If you look at all of my films you'll find an undeniable
> preoccupation with pregnancies, being parents, being children, whether
> to have children. That comes out of a life preoccupation, really … The
> important thing is to try and make a different sort of film within the genre
> and to tell a different kind of story within the overall similarities of the
> discipline. (ibid)

Graham Fuller suggests:

> A Mike Leigh film or play has now become shorthand for a certain kind of domestic scenario, with pop-up toasters and cups of tea, fake-fur coats and rugs, pink bobble carpet slippers, bad haircuts, domestic arguments on leatherette sofas. It evokes a world of china animals, flying geese on brown wallpaper, the smoky pub, the cold light of dawn and cheerless launderettes. Where people live and what they do for a living defines the characters in Leigh's films and plays. They are also characters who are, to a greater or lesser degree, misfits, characters at odds with their environments, their loved ones, their homes and their backgrounds. His films are concerned with that area where upper working class meets lower middle and it has been suggested that they only fully work for those audiences who know about or who live in the social and cultural worlds that his characters inhabit. His films often put forward the idea that to be English is to be locked in a prison where politeness, gaucheness and anxiety about status form constraints which trap people. He choreographs moments of awkwardness and embarrassment, tiny cruelties and failures of communication. There is very little in the way of plot, we are offered the sight of people's curtailed aspirations and case studies in strangulation and frustration – there is often a glimmer of hope that in the web of relationships in which they are caught there could also be a source of strength … humour comes from an acute ear for the ridiculousness of everyday conversations, the hesitancies, repetitions, misunderstandings and silence.

Worksheet 26: Mike Leigh – Film language asks students to examine the film language of a selection of Mike Leigh films and to identify both genre and the construction of realism.

To access student worksheets and other online materials go to *Teaching Stars and Performance* at **www.bfi.org.uk/tfms** and enter User name: **stars@bfi.org.uk** and Password: **te1302sp**.

● Method: the creative process

Bleak Moments (1971), Mike Leigh's first film, was a screen version of a stage play. It was the first substantial outing for his improvisatory compositional technique and among the cast was Alison Steadman who was to become his wife. In a profile of Mike Leigh on the *bfi* website, www.screenonline.org.uk, Richard Dacre says,

> It is a remarkable fact the Mike Leigh completed his second feature film seventeen years after his stunning debut with Bleak Moments in 1971 … the principal reason for this was Leigh's method of production … at the beginning of a project there is no script and once the project has started, the writer-director is irreplaceable – both worrying facts for a financier.

In his interview with Graham Fuller, Mike Leigh explains how he arrived at his methods:

> My job is to gather the resources, then go out there and find the film by making it. But when you discover each element, you pursue or reject it, according to how meaningful you personally think it is. If I had a seminal experience as a student, it wasn't at RADA, where I learned about acting, mostly by default; it wasn't at the London Film School, where I learned the mechanics and basic grammar of film; and it certainly wasn't at the Central School of Arts and Crafts, where I learned how to cut out medieval costumes. It was during the year I spent on the general pre-diploma foundation course at the Camberwell Art School in south London … It had a great figurative drawing tradition, and they were very hot on getting you to look at things properly, to go out with your sketchbook and draw people and buildings. I was in the life drawing class at Camberwell one day when I suddenly had this clairvoyant flash. I realized that what I was experiencing as an art student – and what I most definitely hadn't experienced as an actor – was that working from source and looking at something that actually existed and excited you was the key to making a piece of art. What that gave me as a film-maker, playmaker, storyteller, and as an artist generally, was a sense of freedom. Everything is up for grabs as subject matter if you see it three-dimensionally, and from all possible perspectives, and [if you] are motivated by some kind of feeling about it. I was lucky to unearth this approach to my work because it lets me off one of the main problems in setting up films, that is to say, coming up with a saleable 'good idea' and having to discuss it prematurely …

He adds,

> The rehearsals consist of an accumulation of experienced events; there's a lot of discussion, research and, above all, improvisation. But there are no scenes as such until much later on: they're what I'm concerned with when I come to shooting the film itself. First, there is a journey that leads to the

film, involving elaborate improvisations that create the premise for scenes. I create scenes distilled from improvisation … We do it by going through it and building it up so that it is being written by actually rehearsing.

Mike Leigh goes on to comment on how his approach is put into practice:

… For practical purposes I often work with a notebook in front of me, and my script supervisor writes everything down as an aid … What I do is create the dialogue, the physical action and the subtext all at the same time, as a whole.

… Once I start work, one particular notion or another starts to come into focus – often several. Often one of the things that defines the raw material of what I do is how to spend the money.

Jonathan Romney, commenting on *Secrets and Lies*, says:

One of the pleasures, as ever, in his films is the way Leigh 'gets it right' pinning down all the nuances of behaviour and décor that immediately locate a character socially and emotionally. (The *Guardian*, 23 May 1996)

He describes Mike Leigh's particular mix of comedy and social realism:

… The British suburban landscape at its most mundane is a fascinating terrain that our cinema has hardly begun to explore. There aren't many people who can do Britain this way but when he does, it's like a land mine planted in the heart of sitcom land. (ibid)

In an interview at the National Film Theatre (7 October 2002) with the film critic, Derek Malcolm, Mike Leigh comments further on his methods:

… When I make these films I say 'Come and be in my film. Can't tell you what it's about. I can't tell you what your character is. We'll invent that as part of the process. And you will never know any more than your character knows.' … It's a painstaking process of people getting together and growing. It's a way of building up a world like the real world, with all those tensions. Out of that we … distil things into a structured film …

We work very cautiously in great detail to discuss the palette of the film, the colour and visual spirit of the film in relation to the feeling of the film and what we feel we want to pull out of it …

… Huge numbers of people do live these sorts of lives and I am drawn to deal with them because that's what life is about for a good deal of people.

It is definitely and consistently the case that people love to see a film which reflects their own lives … In the 70s and 80s I didn't make films for cinema but for the television, along with many other filmmakers who were lucky enough to make films. We did films called Play for Today on Monday and Wednesday evenings. People loved them. They had huge viewing figures. They were these kinds of films. People were up for it.

- Discuss these comments with your students. Ask them to consider Jonathan Romney's comments about 'sitcom land'. An interesting area of discussion could be how Leigh's characters compare and contrast with characters from situation comedies.

● Character development: working with actors

Character development is at the centre of Mike Leigh's approach to filmmaking. It remains a fundamental rule in Leigh's ways of working that each actor in any improvisation, or rehearsal, knows only as much about any other character as his or her own character would know in 'real life' at that point in the story. In other words, the films and plays are developed in such a way that the actors do not know what will happen until they have explored and discussed the possibilities in the situation where Leigh has placed the characters. As he says to Fuller:

> Fundamentally my work is about character acting – in the best sense – and social observation. I take it for granted that an actor intimately draws on his own resources and characters. But personally I am not at all disposed to the actor's becoming the character. Apart from the fact that it's bad for your health, it's not creatively constructive. I'm interested in realism but not surrealism.

Leigh's characters come from deep inside his actors and must relate to circumstances with which they are familiar, and at the very least sympathetic … Leigh helps them towards a full realisation of those characters, shaping and manipulating their lines, motivations and emotions, and the overall portrait as the work evolves.

There are discussions and rehearsals, actors are fully involved in the creative process and after the exploratory improvisation period, Leigh writes a structure, indicating the order in which scenes happen often with a single bare sentence, such as, 'Johnny and Sophie meet', 'Betty does Joy's hair', 'Wendy confronts Nicole'. It is then rehearsed and rehearsed until it achieves the required finished quality. There is no such thing in Leigh's work as aimless direction.

Working on Vera Drake

In an interview for *Sight and Sound* (January 2005) on *Vera Drake*, a film about a 1950s' working-class mother, who was a backstreet abortionist, Edward Lawrenson asks Leigh: 'How did the actors get into a 1950 mindset?' Leigh responds:

> During rehearsals we did all the usual things I get people to do which include creating their characters and defining their relationships to one another as well as a massive amount of research. Everyone takes part in this. We talked to people who had memories of that time, we read a lot, we looked at movies and newsreels, we listened to radio programmes,

we consulted a couple of guys at the Imperial War Museum to piece together the characters' journeys through World War II.

Lawrenson quotes Imelda Staunton, who plays Vera Drake:

Working with Mike was shocking, terrifying, exhilarating … But he's right in there next to you. In rehearsal, he doesn't tell you what everyone else is doing, or even what you're going to be doing. We were six months in preparation, creating this woman's entire personal back story from the moment she was born. We recreated Vera's whole war …

Phil Davis, who play's Vera's husband, Stan, says to Lawrenson:

This is my fifth collaboration with Mike. It's really great to get your teeth into something, and really investigate a character … For a feature film, it's unusual to have any rehearsal time at all. In rehearsals and improvisation, you create with him a fictional world which just gets richer and richer the longer you go on. So when Mike comes back with a script it's based on quasi-reality which is already in the DNA of your head, if you like.

Worksheet 27: Mike Leigh – Creating characters offers students the opportunity to develop characters drawn from their own experience.

To access student worksheets and other online materials go to *Teaching Stars and Performance* at **www.bfi.org.uk/tfms** and enter User name: **stars@bfi.org.uk** and Password: **te1302sp**.

Working with stars

As we have discussed, Mike Leigh works in a particular way with actors and often collaborates with them on several projects. Derek Malcolm (2002) asks Mike Leigh about working with Hollywood stars:

DM: Have any Hollywood stars, after the success of Secrets and Lies expressed an interest in working with you?

ML: There are some people like Jennifer Jason Leigh, Willem Defoe and Steve Buscemi, who I know and like and who are 'the American version' of the sort of actors I work with here.

It may be useful to discuss with students what Mike Leigh means by this. What are the differences between these particular actors and 'big' stars such as Julia Roberts and Tom Cruise?

● Mike Leigh and the British film industry

In his interview with Derek Malcolm (2002), Mike Leigh comments on his particular relationship with the British film industry:

> … I only do what all other writers, painters and novelists do. All art is a synthesis of improvisation and order. You put something down and then you work with it … The good thing from my perspective is that nobody puts any pressure on me to say what it's going to be. The backers accept that they don't know what they are going to get …
>
> I can get money but there is a ceiling beyond which people won't take a risk. But that's fine because we make the films we do below that ceiling …

This is exemplified by the funding for *Vera Drake*. Edward Lawrenson discusses with Mike Leigh how he obtained the funding:

> The UK Film Council was in place. And I will simply say that StudioCanal were less than enthusiastic because their previous film with me, *All or Nothing* (2002), though critically reasonably well respected, was on the whole a box office flop. So they were reluctant to take part, though they did put up the money in the end.

Asked whether he feels pressure to make films that will do well at the box office, Leigh comments:

> I've always thought it a good thing if you can make a film that works commercially … But I would be incapable of yielding to manifest pressure to do something I didn't believe in. My most successful film commercially was *Secrets and Lies*, and there's no doubt that was to do with the subject matter – adoption – which has an obvious hook …

However, Leigh is interested in reaching as wide an audience as possible. In his interview with Derek Malcolm (2002), Mike Leigh commented on where his films are shown and who sees them:

> … I am not concerned with making esoteric, obscure kinds of films. These are films that can share and talk to anybody about real things. The good news with *All or Nothing* is that it is being released in the UK by UGC and they are going to put it in multiplexes …

To Graham Fuller (1995) he said,

There's a very strong theatricality and a heightened comic quality in my films, and the business of entertainment is as important to me as anything else.

● Students could discuss to what extent they think Leigh's films have a broad appeal, and which audiences are likely to find his films most appealing.

● Identity and British film

● You could use the following quotations as an interesting basis for discussion of British film and British identity, raising the following questions:
  – Does subject matter define a British film?
  – How many different kinds of films might you describe as British?
  – How might you compare the subject matter or characters in Mike Leigh's films with the themes and characters we discuss in the Hugh Grant case study?

For decades Leigh has been ploughing his own furrow applying his formidable capacity for concentration and focus to developing a body of work. And now, when the British film industry often seems lacking in identity, he has created a film of uncompromising seriousness and self-belief which tackles the most divisive subject conceivable – abortion – yet thus far has united cinema goers of all opinions in admiration for its humanity and strength. (Nick James, in his review of *Vera Drake* in *Sight and Sound*)

And

He's important as a benchmark for what's missing from the rest of the British film industry … Leigh makes unique demands on his actors, requiring them to undertake long sessions of improvisation before the script is finalised and shooting begins and, like Woody Allen, will often reveal to actors … (ibid)

● In the following extract, Mike Leigh points out the contradictions in working in television and film in Britain in the 1970s and 1980s. It may be interesting to discuss with students why he had successes at this time in television but not in film. He suggests that it was partly because of his working methods – they may be able to suggest other reasons.

Graham Fuller discusses with Mike Leigh the problems that working in his particular way brought to his film career:

GF: Tell us about your frustrations at being unable to get a feature made between 1971 and 1987/88:

ML: First of all there was very little feature film-making in Britain from the late sixties to the early eighties. It was alive and well and hiding in television, but you couldn't get indigenous independent feature films made. Then, in my case, I'm the man who doesn't have a script, won't say what's it's going to be about, and doesn't want to discuss casting – not by any standards a viable commercial proposition! The paradox was that, during this long, frustrating period, here I was turning out these telly films, which were immensely popular.

This case study can be useful in helping students to consider:

- Film language
- Methods of acting and directing
- British cinematic traditions and genre
- Exhibition/production of British film
- Britain and Hollywood.

For more material on Mike Leigh, see the transcript of his interview with Michael Coveney, on the British Film Institute website, www.bfi.org.uk. It was part of a retrospective of Mike Leigh's films at the National Film Theatre in November 2005.

Glossary

Auteur

Auteur is the French term for author and is used in film studies which place emphasis/foreground the individual author or director. Although the film's production depends on the collaboration of a group of people auteur theory claims that the director establishes his or her distinct identity or signature across a body of films.

Connote/connotation

The meanings interpreted from a sign (in semiotics this is the signified).

Diegetic/non-diegetic

Referring to the world of a film: diegetic elements are within the film's world. Non-diegetic elements are outside the world of the film. Most commonly used in relation to sound: voiceover and atmospheric music tend to be outside the world of the film (the characters can't hear them).

Genre

Theoretical term for classification of media texts into types. This is often identifiable by a repeated pattern of iconography such as setting, props and costume.

Hegemony

Concept (constructed by Italian thinker, Gramsci) referring to power achieved by the dominant resulting from persuading the subordinate that arrangements are in their interest. The elite is allowed to rule because the rest of the population allows it to do so.

Icon/iconic

A sign that works through resembling something. It can be defined by the dominant signs which signify a particular person or object, eg, Charlie Chaplin might be defined by his moustache, bowler hat and cane or a Western may be defined through landscapes, the dress of the actors, guns and so on.

Iconography

The study of familiar iconic signs or elements within a genre/across a body of films, eg, the physical attributes and dress of actors, the settings and other elements such as the landscape, the guns, the saloon bar in the Western.

Ideological, ideology

A body of ideas and understanding about the social world and how these ideas are related to the distribution of power in society. Dominant ideologies are often perceived as 'common sense' beliefs.

Indexical

A sign that works by a specific relationship to the object or concept it refers to, eg, smoke is an indication of fire.

Intertextuality

Aspects of a media text which can be understood by reference to another text; meaning is created though referencing the audience's knowledge of other media texts.

Mediation

The process by which a media text represents an idea, person, issue or event to the audience. Things undergo change in the process of being acted upon by the media.

Mise en scène

A French term which means 'putting together the scene'. It is used in textual analysis for the combination of visual elements within the frame.

Montage

From the French word meaning to edit, it means the assembling of footage to form a whole. In Film Studies it often refers to the system of editing used by the Soviet filmmakers of the 1920s.

Oligopoly

An industry controlled by a small number of producers.

Paradigm

A relationship 'across' a set of elements of the same type.

Representation

The way that issues, events, groups and images are reconstructed through media texts.

Semiotics

The study of signs and sign systems.

Spectator

In film theory the spectator is constructed and addressed by the text. The word is often used for 'audience'.

Transparency

The way in which the construction of media texts is 'invisible' and are presented as natural.

Vertically integrated

A business activity involving one company acquiring others elsewhere (either earlier or later) in the chain of the production process, eg, production, distribution and exhibition in the film industry.

Voyeurism

The act of viewing individuals without their knowledge.

References and resources

Bibliography

K Anger (1975), *Hollywood Babylon*, Arrow Books Limited

P Cook and M Bernink (1999), *The Cinema Book*, 2nd Edition, bfi

M Coveney (1996), *The World According to Mike Leigh*, HarperCollins

R Dyer (1998), *Stars*, bfi

E Dyja (2004), *Film and Television Handbook*, bfi

B Gallagher, 'Some Historical Reflections on the Paradoxes of Stardom in the American Film Industry', www.imagesjournal.com

C Gledhill and L Williams (2000), *Reinventing Film Studies*, Hodder Education

S Hall (1978), *Policing the Crisis: mugging, the state and law and order*, Macmillan

S Hayward (1996), *Key Concepts in Cinema Studies*, Routledge

J Hollows and M Jancovich (1995), *Approaches to Popular Film*, Manchester University Press

M Leigh (1995), Naked *and Other Screenplays*, Faber and Faber

R Maltby (1995), *Hollywood Cinema*, Blackwell Publishers

R Murphy (1992), *Sixties British Cinema*, bfi

D Lusted and P Drummond (1985), *TV and Schooling*, Routledge

P McDonald (2000), *The Star System: Hollywood's Production of Popular Identities*, Wallflower Press

J Naremore (1988), *Acting in Cinema*, University of California Press

J Nelmes (1996), *An Introduction to Film Studies*, Routledge

P Powrie, A Davies, B Babington (2004), *The Trouble with Men*, Wallflower Press

T Schatz (1996), *The Genius of the System*, Faber and Faber

A Spicer (2004), 'The Reluctance to Commit: Hugh Grant and the New British Romantic Comedy' in *The Trouble with Men*, P Powrie et al

J Staiger (1995), *The Studio System*, Rutgers University Press

L Stern (2002), 'Putting on a Show, or the Ghostliness of Gesture', www.sensesofcinema.com/contents/02/21sd_s

S Street (1997), *British National Cinema*, Routledge

M Sweet (2005), *Shepperton Babylon*, Faber and Faber

D Thomson (2005), *The Whole Equation, A History of Hollywood*, Little, Brown

J Wyatt (1994), *High Concept: Movies and Marketing in Hollywood*,
  University of Texas Press

Useful websites

www.bfi.org.uk – website with many useful links and resources

www.filmunlimited.co.uk – The Guardian's film resources

www.imagesjournal.com – useful articles and features

www.imdb.co.uk – Internet Movie Database

www.oscars.com – website with details of winners and speeches

www.sensesofcinema.com – useful website with wide range of articles and
  directors

Selected filmography

About a Boy (Chris and Paul Weitz, UK/USA, 2002)

All About Eve (Joseph L Mankiewicz, USA, 1950)

All About My Mother (Todo sobre mi madre) (Pedro Almodóvar, Spain/France,
1999)

All or Nothing (Mike Leigh GB/France, 2002)

Angels with Dirty Faces (Michael Curtiz, USA, 1938)

Armageddon (Michael Bay, USA, 1998)

The Bad and the Beautiful (Vincente Minnelli, USA, 1952)

The Band Wagon (Vincente Minnelli, USA, 1953)

Batman (Tim Burton, USA, 1989)

Bridget Jones's Diary (Sharon Maguire, 2001)

Broken Blossoms (D W Griffiths, USA, 1919)

Bulldog Drummond (F Richard Jones, USA, 1929)

Charlie's Angels (McG, USA, 2000)

Con Air (Simon West, USA, 1997)

Die Hard (John McTiernan, USA, 1988),

Extreme Measures (Michael Apted, USA, 1996)

Face/Off (John Woo, USA, 1997)

42nd Street (Lloyd Bacon, USA, 1933)

Four Weddings and a Funeral (Mike Newell, UK, 1994)

The Full Monty (Peter Cattaneo, USA/UK 1997)

Gangs of New York (Martin Scorsese, USA, 2002)

Gladiator (Ridley Scott, USA, 2000),

Gone with the Wind (Victor Fleming, USA, 1939)
The Good Girl (Miguel Arteta, USA/Germany/Netherlands, 2002)
Henry V (Laurence Olivier, UK, 1944)
In Which We Serve (David Lean, Noel Coward, UK, 1942)
Kes (Kenneth Loach, GB, 1969)
Living in Oblivion (Tom DiCillo, USA, 1995)
Life Is Sweet (Mike Leigh, GB, 1990)
Lock Stock and Two Smoking Barrels (Guy Ritchie, UK, 1998)
The Man Who Knew Too Much (Alfred Hitchcock, USA, 1956)
The Matrix (Andy and Larry Wachowski, USA, 1999)
The Men (Fred Zinneman, USA, 1950)
Millions Like Us (Sydney Gilliat and Frank Launder, UK, 1943)
Morvern Callar (Lynne Ramsay, UK/Can, 2001)
Nine Months (Chris Columbus, USA, 1995)
Notting Hill (Roger Michell, UK/USA, 1999)
Once Upon a Time in the Midlands (Shane Meadows, UK/Germany/Netherlands, 2002)
On the Waterfront (Elia Kazan, USA, 1954)
Opening Night (John Cassavetes, USA, 1977)
The Player (Robert Altman, USA, 1992)
Pulp Fiction (Quentin Tarantino, USA, 1994)
Pride and Prejudice (Joe Wright, US/UK/France, 2005)
Raging Bull (Martin Scorsese, USA, 1980)
Rear Window (Alfred Hitchcock, USA, 1954)
Rebel Without a Cause (Nicholas Ray, USA, 1955)
The Red Shoes (Michael Powell, Emeric Pressburger, UK, 1948)
A Room for Romeo Brass (Shane Meadows, UK/Canada, 1999)
Secrets and Lies (Mike Leigh, UK, 1996)
Singin' in the Rain (Gene Kelly and Stanley Donen, USA, 1952)
Sunset Boulevard (Billy Wilder, USA, 1950)
This Happy Breed (David Lean, UK, 1944)
Titanic (James Cameron, USA, 1997)
Top Gun (Tony Scott, USA, 1986)
Vertigo (Alfred Hitchcock, USA, 1958)
White Heat (Raoul Walsh, USA, 1949)

Acknowledgements

To my parents for our Friday nights at the Muswell Hill Odeon.

To my own dear family – Ian, Anna and Minnie without whom this book would have been finished a great deal sooner.